PELICAN BOOK A636

The Contemporary Cinema

PENELOPE HOUSTON

Penelope Houston, who was born in Kensington, was
educated at Roedean School and Somerville College,
Oxford, where she read modern history just after the war.
While at Oxford she wrote film reviews for *Isis*, the undergraduate magazine, and was associated, as one of three co-
editors, with the independent film magazine, *Sequence*.
After leaving Oxford she worked for a year as a research
assistant on the official *History of the War*. She joined the
staff of the British Film Institute in 1950, as associate editor,
and became general editor of the Institute's publications in
1956. She has edited *Sight and Sound*, the film quarterly
published by the Institute, since 1956, and also serves on the
editorial board of *Contrast*, the Institute's television quarterly. She has from time to time contributed articles to a
number of newspapers and magazines.

D1188868

The Contemporary Cinema

by Penelope Houston

With thirty-two plates

Penguin Books

Penguin Books Ltd, Harmondsworth, Middlesex, England
Penguin Books Inc., 3300 Clipper Mill Road, Baltimore 11, Md, U.S.A.
Penguin Books Pty Ltd, Ringwood, Victoria, Australia

First published 1963
Reprinted 1964

Made and printed in Great Britain by Cox and Wyman Ltd,
London, Reading, and Fakenham
Set in Monotype Imprint

Contents

Preface

This book does not pretend to be a history of the cinema – hardly even a history of that particularly urgent quarter of the cinema's total existence contained in the years since the war. History ought to be recollected, if not in tranquillity, at least at some distance from the event; and the starting-point of this survey is the confused, exciting, stimulating, and essentially paradoxical situation of the cinema today. More people now watch more film, in the cinema and on television, than ever before. About half the population of this country never actually enter a cinema; yet they accept film, in one form or another, as an unquestioned part of their lives. The fight for peaceful co-existence with television has undeniably weakened Western cinemas industrially. And, at the same time, there have been few periods in film history of greater creative excitement, greater opportunities for artists who want to use the screen for personal statement. Television, it could be argued, is in the process of liberating the cinema. Whether directors such as Michelangelo Antonioni and Ingmar Bergman, Alain Resnais and François Truffaut, have created their audience through their work, or whether the presence of the audience helps to en- courage the film-makers, is both arguable and unanswerable.

The fact is that audience and films are there; and even a phrase like minority cinema takes on a new meaning when the B.B.C. transmits films such as de Sica's *Bicycle Thieves* or Andrzej Wajda's trilogy of wartime Poland to audiences of seven or eight million.

What influences have affected the attitudes of film-makers, audiences, and critics; through what processes has the confident, solid cinema of twenty years ago evolved into the cinema as we know and experience it today? What happens next? These are some of the questions that confront one. The period covered by this book – the post-war years – more or less coincides with that of my own involvement with the cinema, as interested onlooker, as critic, and as editor of a film magazine; and one necessarily sees this still-young art in the context of one's own generation, so that no one whose real introduction to the medium's possibilities came at the time of Welles's *Citizen Kane* can have quite the same attitudes as the filmgoer who grew up with silent movies. Writing about this problematical mixture of art and industry one is always aware, too, of how many different approaches might be equally valid. The literary critic doesn't have to bother with such things as changes in reading habits or a rise in the cost of printing ink. But no one who writes about the cinema can afford for too long to ignore what it costs to make a film, or where and how it must look for its audience.

I have tried here to hold a balance, to relate what appears on the screen to the circumstances of its production, and to see how the world's various industries confront their separate problems. The object has been to provide a commentary on a period, to indicate a framework and a context, rather than to analyse specific films in detail; and I have had to leave out of account whole areas of film-making (the animated cinema, for instance, or the film as applied to science and industry) with what amount to histories of their own. It is the problem of the creative process, the question of how and why films are made the way they are, that the commentator can try to illuminate, endeavouring to interpret where he can.

I would like to thank my colleagues at the British Film Institute, in particular Miss Norah Traylen, Miss Brenda Davies, Miss Sylvia Loeb, and Mr Richard Roud, for invaluable help with the illustrations and documentation. I am especially grateful to Mr Tom Milne, who chose the stills with me, and to Mr John Gillett, who did most of the work on the check-list of films and directors. Without the Institute's resources as a whole, the book would probably have remained unwritten.

P.H.

Illustrations are reproduced by courtesy of: British Lion Films, Columbia Pictures, Compton Cameo, Contemporary Films, Curzon Film Distributors, Daiei, Film Polski, Gala Film Distributors, Gianni Bufardi, Golden Era Films, Metro-Goldwyn-Mayer, Miracle Films, Mondial Films, National Film Archive, Paramount Pictures, Producciones Angel, Rank Film Distributors, Sebricon, Toho Company, Twentieth Century-Fox, United Artists, Warner-Pathé, Woodfall Film Productions.

1. Introductory

Films or movies, the pictures or motion pictures: even the choice of word reaches out tentatively towards the definition of an attitude. 'Film' is neutral; 'movies' ought to be fun; 'the pictures' means a double-feature and a choc-ice; 'motion picture' is American and assertive, suggesting an Academy Awards ceremony or a graduate thesis on 'the medium'. Entertainment, art, mass communication; industry, private experiment, public service; the most important of the arts, in terms of twentieth-century society, or an art only on sufferance; the one art whose production can take place in factory conditions, or an industry with an art locked within it, perpetually struggling to break free. The sweeping definitions could be almost indefinitely extended: 'seventh art', 'tenth muse', 'opium for the masses'. Call it all these, and then come back again to the cinema. And 'that which makes the cinema', said René Clair forty years or so ago, 'is not to be discussed.'

It is only during the last few years, however, that a new definition has crept into the list: the mass medium in danger of losing its mass audience. To look back to 1946, in Britain, is to remember a popular cinema which is never likely to come again. Over thirty million cinema tickets were sold each week. At the roundabouts on the arterial roads leading out of London the big grey Odeons stood guard, forbidding blockhouses in the heavy thirties style. Andy Hardy and Old Mother Riley, Abbott and Costello and the Bowery Boys, Tarzan and Blondie kept 'the pictures' turning over. Now only the indestructible Tarzan remains, the last survivor from the age of innocence.

Over the intervening years, 'the pictures' have been losing ground steadily to 'film', and the Odeons have become filling stations or factories or dance-halls. A habit has disintegrated, for the most part unregretted, and if the sociologists' interest has appeared only mildly aroused it is probably because the shift has been one of emphasis and situation rather than more fundamentally of public taste. 'Coronation Street' now nets in two evenings two-thirds or more of that weekly thirty million; even 'Tonight' collects about a quarter of it. Television has become the routine, borrowing wholesale from the cinema the comedy series and Westerns and thrillers, the habit-forming programmes. The new habit has attracted all the sociological attention, while the old one has been allowed quietly to decline. And decline it has. By 1962, according to a Board of Trade estimate, the cinema audience in Britain was down to about eight million a week, while six years had seen the closing down of more than a third of the nation's cinemas.

The pattern has been found to repeat itself in almost every country with an expanding television service. And, as each cinema industry in turn laboriously discovers for itself, there are other counter-attractions. Cinema managers in America, then in Britain, more recently in France, have voiced their complaints in almost identical terms: too many cars (*la motorisation*, say the French, will be the death of the cinema); too many other things for people to do with their time. An industry which had encouraged its audience to regard it as a habit, to queue at the same time each week for a film as much like last week's as possible, to buy cinema as unthinkingly as it bought toothpaste or cigarettes, discovered with a deep sense of shock and affront that the wares it had been selling for so long as necessities were suddenly being treated as luxuries. The nightly switch-on replaces the weekly visit to the pictures: only the cinema manager can be said really to regret it.

But, of course – and it is by no means a paradox – a declining audience need not also mean a less enthusiastic one. The Pilkington Report, in another context, has nailed the fallacy of claiming to gauge public taste on a purely statistical basis. People watch television, as they used to go to the movies, not to see *something*, but to see *anything*. A mass audience brings its own apathy, and the fact that a vast number of people are watching the same thing does not prove that they are enjoying themselves, merely that they are there. The rebellion of the docile and tractable audience of fifteen years ago forced the entertainment cinema to change its strategy. It has discovered that any picture aimed purposefully enough at the big commercial market (a *Ben-Hur* or a *South Pacific*, a *Longest Day* or a *Dr No*) will make at least as much money as it would have done fifteen years ago, and probably a good deal more. Movies must emphasize their difference from each other, not their similarities; selling becomes a series of shrill demands for public attention. But if the selling is right, then, unmistakably and even enthusiastically, the audience is there. And, at the same time, there has never been a larger, more wide-awake, or more interested public for the kind of film which only a few years ago would have seemed desperately specialized. The distributors who acquired *L'Avventura* or *L'Année dernière à Marienbad* or *Shadows* knew what they were about: yesterday's defiant risk becomes today's cocktail-party talking-point.

This cinema has become fashionable – sometimes to an extent dangerous for its own good. Directors' reputations go up and down as rapidly as speculative shares. Buy blue-chip Bergmans in 1959 and Antonionis in 1961; watch the continental festivals for the next hot tip, the next director whose work will be talked up, written up, photographed for the glossies, before most people have even got around to seeing it for themselves. Film magazines all over the world weigh in with articles which uncover the same new trends at the same time: when the trends turn out to be not quite what was expected, the disillusionment comes as abruptly as the discovery. New directors are continually being told that they are betraying a promise they never knew they had shown: behind them, the next new wave is already thundering up the beach. In this atmosphere, which makes for liveliness if not for stability, the queues swing over from the Odeons to the specialized cinemas, the Hollywood talents are scattered to the winds of Europe, and Hollywood itself no longer looks like the capital of the cinema, but the Park Avenue of the American television industry.

In the immediate post-war years, specialized cinemas were few in number and relatively regular in their clientele. Now they are all over the place, and the number of people who would never think of going to see a film in a foreign language falls away every year. The reason, perhaps, is not only that the specialized film is more readily accessible than it ever used to be, but also that the cinema has found its responsive public because it can be taken so thoroughly for granted. A generation has grown up with the sound film, with colour, with the whole vocabulary of the screen. The old critical battlefields – Can movies properly be called an art at all? Are silent films intrinsically better than the talkies? Are big screens a dead loss creatively? – are deserted. No one any longer has to have close-ups and flashbacks defined for them, to be told in basic terms how the movies work. The syntax of the moving image (film *or* television) has become one of the integral, unquestioned things in everyone's experience.

So experiment becomes that much easier. And this whole atmosphere, with its hints of creative possibility, has made the cinema – or at any rate the European cinema – a more stimulating place to work in. But there have also been heavy casualties, most obviously in the decline of the Hollywood empires, those power symbols of the international cinema. Hollywood domination at its worst may have seem brutalized, a bronze idol which took out its human sacrifice in talent; but at its best, it afforded its own kind of stability. There was confidence, because there was continuity. A studio could take the time to let young artists and actors develop, sure that it would still be there when the time came round to get the best out of them. Orson Welles spent the better part of his first year at R.K.O. watching films, and then emerged to direct *Citizen Kane*. This could hardly happen now: the ballast that kept the whole thing afloat has gone, along with all the average, unpretentious, easy-going movies which were never intended to do more than provide the audience with a way of passing the time, the studios which promoted them with a steady income, and the people who made them with a means of exercising their craft.

Production investment touches fantastic levels. Even the rights to *My Fair Lady* change hands at more than $5,000,000, while every news bulletin on *Cleopatra* quoted a slightly higher figure, a few more millions on a production budget which has been estimated at anything between $30,000,000 and $40,000,000. To get back the kind of money that is being spent on them, some of these films have not only to be best-sellers in the normal sense but to join the ten or twenty top-sellers in the whole of cinema history. So the production investment is hedged around with safeguards, in the form of the right cast, the right big-screen system, the right sales campaign. It is all a good deal more like launching a battleship, one director has said, than making a film. It has to be.

Only the American industry, with its world market, internationally known stars, and long-term experience, can readily afford the kind of investment involved in one of the superspectacles. For Europe and the Eastern cinemas the best chances lie in films of moderate cost which can get back their expenses within a limited market, and in productions whose quality breaks down the international barriers. So the cinema of the sixties presents its own form of split personality: the big and the small; the expensive and the cheap; the very safe and the very daring – success can lie at either end of the scale, but is unlikely to be found too near the middle.

Trash sells faster than ever, but it has to be exploitable, sensational trash. So the nudist films, the cut-price horror films, the censor-free club cinemas trading on the dismal delights of the supposedly illicit, come and go. *My Bare Lady* and *Some Like It Nude* compete with *The White Slavers* and *Juvenile Passion*. At a rather higher level, fashion goes in waves and extremism flourishes. Uncertain of its public, the film industry will try anything once and most things more than once. And the cinema, consequently, becomes more tense and nervous, an excitable industry which has not quite come to terms with its own reduced circumstances. But if this applies, in general terms, to America and Western Europe, on the other side of the world newer industries are still developing, still unassailed by television and the other competitors, still able to find audiences open to experience at a simpler level.

This is just part of the pattern of contemporary cinema, that relation of the audience to the industry which determines so much of what we see on the screen. It is a strikingly different picture from the one confronting Roger Manvell when, during the war, he wrote his famous Pelican *Film*, the book which must have started so many of his juniors along the road to the cinema. Then Hollywood still dominated, the Italian cinema had hardly begun to shake off the deadening weight of Fascism, the Indian and Japanese industries remained more or less unknown quantities, and the cinemas of the West had no problems about where to look for an audience. Although the cinema already had more than forty years of history behind it, its critical literature was not much more than twenty years old and its historians had formed their theories in the days before sound. The last two decades have seen an enormous accumulation of experience, with ideas about the cinema shifting and expanding to match what the screen shows us. The cinema of Antonioni, Resnais, Godard, Mizoguchi, Welles influences our ideas about the past as well as the future.

Too young to have acquired its academic traditions, old enough to feel the need for them, the cinema remains an art in search of a history. The popular art lives in the present; and the cinema, which has been above all a means of expression for the myths and dreams of this century, has also been the art of the present tense, of images which on the screen are always happening *now*, as we watch. For this reason among others, the film critic is perhaps especially susceptible to the influence of the climate in which he is writing. Our feelings about what the screen can do alter as we see what it is doing.

At the moment, for instance, the Western cinema looks a great deal less like a mass medium than it did twenty years ago. Does this mean, in effect, that television has assumed some of its duties? In the thirties, Arthur Elton and Edgar Anstey made a celebrated documentary called *Housing Problems*, an exposé of living conditions in the slums of Britain. Now, if only in terms of the audience reached and the impact made, a single item in 'Panorama' would do an infinitely more effective propaganda job than a film, and give as well that absolute conviction of here and now which is television's special advantage over the cinema.

Since cinema is no longer *the* mass medium – and at some moments looks a little shaky about its own future as *a* mass medium – the attitudes of the artists who work in it and the critics who write about it are bound, directly or indirectly, consciously or unconsciously, to be affected. One of the more wide-spread tenets of film criticism, recently restated by Siegfried Kracauer in his book *Nature of Film* (1961), is that realist cinema is the best and truest cinema: 'Films are true to the medium to the extent that they penetrate the world before our eyes.' Cinema began in observation, with Lumière's train pulling into that distant station, yet within a few years Georges Méliès was demonstrating where fantasy might take it. The cinema of fact and that of fancy, the cinema which observes and the cinema which imagines, continually co-exist and overlap. There is no morality of art which can validly determine that one type of film has more 'right' on its side than another.

There is, of course, a strong pull towards realism, to the use of the camera as a recording instrument, as there is a continual impulse towards the role of social historian. A nation's films reflect a nation's thoughts. And through the post-war history of the Italian cinema, more distinctly than any other country's, comes the transition from one way of thinking to another, one form of realism to another. Neo-realism, that great aspiration of the late forties, influenced everyone who thought about films. The movement, considered collectively, probably remains the most influential single force in post-war cinema. But it belonged very specifically to its time, just as the Italian cinema of recent years is demonstratively contemporary. If *L'Avventura* now seems more relevant, more of our time, even more 'real' than *Bicycle Thieves*, this is partly because a decade or so of film-making has changed some ideas about screen realism, as about the cinema itself. The cinema advances through the questions its artists put to themselves; and the Italians, in the late forties and again in the early sixties, have been asking many of the right questions.

2. The Italian Experience

The reality buried under the myths slowly reflowered. The cinema began its creation of the world. Here was a tree; here an old man; here a house; here a man eating, a man sleeping, a man crying. . . .

The quotation is from Cesare Zavattini, scriptwriter of most of de Sica's films, one of the most fertile creative minds in the post-war Italian cinema, and a man whose ideas about the cinema and about society run easily in double harness. Do away with the story, said Zavattini, hunt down your material in the streets around you, take the simplest of human situations and uncover the elements contained within it; do away with the professional actor, since 'to want one person to play another implies the calculated plot'; and do away with the kind of technical paraphernalia that gets in the way of this immediate contact with reality. Years ago, Zavattini recorded a conversation he had had with an American producer. '*We* show a plane flying over,' said the American. 'A gun fires, the plane crashes. And this is how *you* imagine it. The plane passes by. . . . The plane passes by again. . . . The plane passes by once more.' Certainly, said Zavattini, but this doesn't take us far enough: 'we must make it pass by twenty times.'

Everyday living, in its most familiar, unadventurous guises, can never be boring. Drama which tries to impose a plot on 'life' is falsification. These were the standards Zavattini raised. A woman buying a pair of shoes; an old man nodding on a park bench; a girl getting up in the morning (the maid-servant in *Umberto D*): these are some subjects for the cinema, and an ideal would be to record an hour or two in any man's life. Zavattini himself, no doubt, also recognized this to be pointless in one sense and impossible in another. Merely to keep the camera turning is meaningless; yet the minute the artist begins to cut, to select, to discipline his material, he is exposing his own attitudes and responses. 'Life' and what the film makes of it are bound to be two different things, just as to watch an aircraft flying overhead twenty times would be the most boring experience conceivable, if that really was all that we were seeing.

Like many practitioners who also theorize about their craft, Zavattini produced conflicting ideas both about what neo-realism *was* and about what he would have liked it to be. His best scripts have been artfully worked out, with leanings towards sentimentality; some of his theorizing has been so austere as to suggest that for him all cinema ought to aspire to the condition of factual reporting. But if neo-realism never meant in practice quite what Zavattini said it ought to mean, the actual achievement remained substantial enough. 'The most important attempts of liberal man to realize himself in film,' one critic has grandly said. The movement came out of an unpromising cinema, at an unlikely time. Mussolini's régime had established the Centro Sperimentale, the film training-school in Rome, but had not permitted its graduates creative freedom. Italian films had moved from their so-called 'white telephone' era, of theatrical intrigues among the potted palms of a hundred grand hotels, into a period of militant propaganda. Then, in 1942 and 1943, several things happened. Umberto Barbaro, a critic and teacher at the Centro Sperimentale, wrote an attack on the conventions of Italian film-making, in which the word neo-realism was used; Luchino Visconti, who before the war had been an assistant to the great French director Jean Renoir, made his first feature, *Ossessione*; and Michelangelo Antonioni, a young film journalist, shot a documentary, *Il Gente del Po*, which, he has since said, 'really did go some way towards anticipating the neo-realist films'.

There are other contestants for this honour, though critical opinion traditionally gives pride of place to *Ossessione*. Taking for his raw material James M. Cain's novel *The Postman Always Rings Twice* (an act of piracy which meant that for copyright reasons the film could not for years be publicly shown abroad), Visconti adapted it to an Italian setting. The long Italian roads, the countryside around Ferrara, the little town in the sunshine, the roadside café which becomes the lovers' prison, and from which they look out at the landscape of freedom: through these settings, as three-dimensional as any in the cinema, the Italians learnt that they had acquired a director who would show them something harsh, unlovely, and honest about their own country. As melodrama, *Ossessione* has all that thunderstorm quality of tension and electric energy appropriate in a first work by a film-maker who has placed himself among the cinema's natural autocrats. Miles away from Zavattini's world, it belongs to another conception of realism. But if its connexions seem, as the years go by, to be with the rest of Visconti's work rather than with the record of neo-realism, *Ossessione* still pointed the way forward through its awareness of place and time.

Ossessione, however, was to remain for several years an unknown film, one of the cinema's many rumoured but unseen masterpieces. It was through Rossellini and de Sica that British and American audiences first discovered neo-realism; and the quality of excitement roused by a film such as the former's *Rome, Open City* was also a part of the whole rediscovery of a newly awakened Italy. Rossellini had graduated from documentary to official war films. Then, with the Germans hardly out of Rome, he set out to get down on the screen this story of resistance action and Gestapo reprisals. The actual film stock was of indifferent quality; shooting conditions were such that the film looked as raw and rough as it felt. Even on its own terms, *Open City* has all kinds of limitations, many of them apparent enough at the time. But here were the streets of Rome, and Anna Magnani forcing her vigorous way through them. Here was all the insistent conviction of the real thing, after years of the Hollywood resistance movie, with its bogus accents and brave little gestures and studio mock-ups of European towns.

After the explosion, a slight lull. Rossellini's *Paisà* (1946) already looked less impressive. It took a series of episodes in the Italian war, moving a stage northwards with each one, to end with a moving episode of a massacre of partisans fighting in the Italian lakes, but it lacked *Open City*'s voracious immediacy. The stories were no more than anecdotes; and the mixture of actuality and contrivance, with the sad little ironies so carefully worked out and so roughly narrated, began to jar. James Agee, writing in the *Nation*, had a discerning comment on a director who for many critics could then do no wrong: '. . . a sickening lack of mental firmness, of fundamental moral aliveness, and of taste; but at his best an extremely vigorous talent for improvisation, for naturalistic poetry and for giving the illusion of the present tense.'

'The illusion of the present tense': this, to begin with, was what neo-realism seemed to mean. The cinema had been liberated from its studios; the film-makers were out in the streets and the fields, bringing together professional and non-professional actors, putting their country's experience on record. Affectionately (as in Luigi Zampa's *Vivere in Pace*, an undistinguished film which enjoyed a great vogue), luridly (as in

Giuseppe de Santis's *Caccia Tragica*), energetically (as in Renato Castellani's *Sotto il Sole di Roma*) they built a national cinema out of their own recent history. Behind the films could be sensed a driving urge to get it on to the screen, and in doing so to rehabilitate a national reputation. In Vittorio de Sica's *Shoeshine* (1946), a sympathetic eye was turned on another familiar problem: two boys drawn into crime, victims of war, of institutionalism, of self-betrayal. De Sica's film has been unavailable for so long in this country that it has been overshadowed in critical estimation by *Bicycle Thieves*, made two years later. But in *Shoeshine* (as, indeed, in the wartime *I Bambini ci guardano*) the director's emotional sympathies were at full stretch, his attitude to film-making clearly outlined.

In an international critics' poll organized by *Sight and Sound* in 1952, *Bicycle Thieves* was voted as the best film ever made; in a similar poll held ten years later, it had dropped to sixth place. Clearly, it is not by a long way the greatest film in cinema history; arguably, it may not even be de Sica's finest work. But it is a film so thoroughly committed to its characters, made with such transparent resolution and devotion, that its continuing hold on people's imagination seems self-explanatory. *Bicycle Thieves* took us a step towards Zavattini's ideal cinema, in the sense not only that it used non-professional actors, real places, and a sufficiently basic problem (the search for a bicycle which also means a livelihood), but that it put film-making very directly to the service of social comment.

Of course *Bicycle Thieves* is sentimental; which is to say that the director and writer find it easier to respond to a child's loneliness than to a hard economic fact – or perhaps believe that the loneliness and the economics can be equated. It is the child rather than the stolen bicycle, and the child in fact rather than the child as symbol, that people remember from the film, along with the pressure of the Roman streets, the sense of isolation in a crowding city, and the melancholy strangeness of the city

23

itself. *Bicycle Thieves* speaks most clearly when it takes the point of view of a frightened child, just as *Umberto D*, which de Sica and Zavattini made four years later, works through the experience of a frightened old man. By this time, however, there was an audible note of self-pity. The moral concern remained as sharp as ever, and the film felt less need than *Bicycle Thieves* to dramatize its incidents. Scenes such as the famous one of the servant girl getting up in the morning take life at its own pace and on its own terms: an unstressed reality is enough. All the same, one cannot feel quite as much concern for Umberto D., the old pensioner struggling to preserve his pathetic dignity, as de Sica demands.

In between, de Sica had made the likeable fable *Miracle in Milan*, in which the city outcasts, living in their tumbledown shanty-town on a strip of derelict waste-land, come into baffling contact with a caricatured world of big business when oil is struck beneath their settlement. De Sica sends his innocents on a broomstick flight to a better world; for on earth they are the dispossessed. And dispossession, essentially, has been his theme. He set out to become the poet of the unemployed and the unemployable, the lost and the homeless, the victims of a society which may be caricatured (as in *Miracle in Milan*), or humanized (as in *Umberto D*), or simply felt as a force exerting irresistible pressure (as in *Bicycle Thieves*). It is not surprising that children play such a part in his films, that he has never got as far with adult relationships, between equals, as he has with protective ones (father and son in *Bicycle Thieves*, mother and daughter in *Two Women*, old man and young servant in *Umberto D*).

Such themes demand an absolute purity of feeling, and a directness of technique which can strike to the heart of a situation and persuade us that we are seeing nothing but the truth. When suggestions of patronage creep in (as in *Il Tetto*), when the director applies elementary shock tactics to force an emotional reaction (as in *Two Women*), one feels that he can no longer trust his own responses. From concentrated observation he moves to a series of jottings, from sentiment to sentimentality. De Sica had been an actor long before he came to direct, and as his own playing, in other men's films, has grown more florid, more shrewdly loaded in its application of Italian charm, so his sensibilities as a film-maker seem to have become blunted. The child and his father in *Bicycle Thieves*, sitting on the edge of a pavement in a hostile city, alone and self-sufficient, form our image of de Sica's cinema; not the shot at the end of *Two Women* when the camera pulls back from Sophia Loren and her daughter, two carefully framed figures all too dolefully and self-consciously mourning their lost innocence.

It would have been in the nature of a miracle, given the conditions of film-making, if de Sica and Zavattini had been able to sustain the purity of their vision. Almost from the moment that the word neo-realism became common usage, in fact, the artists concerned began insisting that the movement itself was a spent force. The Italian government and tourist industry had never encouraged these sombre images of poverty and desolation; the Roman public queued for Rita Hayworth rather than *Bicycle Thieves*, so that the film-makers could count neither on official nor popular support. And meanwhile the international success of *Bitter Rice*, with Silvana Mangano waist-deep in the mud of the rice fields, had helped another brand of Italian cinema on its way. Lollobrigida and Loren rode donkeys up hilly village streets and were chased across the marshes; de Sica enjoyed himself as a jovial country policeman; Fernandel came from France to play opposite Gino Cervi in a string of comedies about a priest and a Communist. A left-wing cinema, committed to the cause of the disinherited, had little prospect of competing with Loren and Lollobrigida.

The uncompromising masterpiece, however, had been made before this. Luchino Visconti, after directing *Ossessione*, had worked for several years in the theatre. Then, in 1948, he came back to the cinema, went to Sicily with a film unit, and directed a picture originally intended as the first part of a never-completed trilogy: *La Terra Trema*. Its subject was a family of fishermen, victims of a crushing economic system and of fate itself, falling slowly apart under the strain of poverty yet fighting every inch of the way. At the end, stripped to their self-respect, they still look, said the French critic André Bazin, like Renaissance princes.

La Terra Trema makes no concessions. It is long, slow, and sometimes none too clear in its course of action. It can be boring, if with a kind of majestic, self-induced monotony. Since Visconti used an entirely amateur cast, recruited on the spot, and encouraged them to make up their own dialogue and follow their own rhythms of speech, the Sicilian dialect left even an Italian audience at a loss. Not at all surprisingly, in spite of its international reputation, *La Terra Trema* remains a film more talked about than seen, outside the world of the film society and National Film Theatre audiences.

But its importance, not only in the context of neo-realism, comes from its absolute interlocking of social and human themes. The family are moulded by the life they have led, by the history of their village; their opponents, the men of the fish-market, are themselves caught up in a system of exploitation of which they are not the makers. Step by step we are led towards a Marxist solution, which is not contained within the film, because, evidently, the fishermen were not ready for cooperative action. So Visconti was called defeatist by sections of the Italian left, when in fact part of the film's value lies in its refusal to impose its own answer. The whole work has a bleak self-sufficiency, with its formal rhythm, its mobile camera, its total awareness of a world restricted to the crumbling houses of Acitrezza, the beach, the fish-market, the sea beyond the knife-edge rocks. When the family finally goes down in defeat, the effect is of tragedy barely touched by pathos. We can feel sorry for the people of *Bicycle Thieves* but not for these Sicilians, since the film leaves us, as audience, outside.

This formidable picture, admitting the grandeur as well as the misery of aspiration defeated, yielded no real sequel, from Visconti or anyone else. Visconti went on to make in *Bellissima*, with Anna Magnani, a satisfyingly ironic slice-of-life drama. Then came the Stendhalian *Senso*, shot in ravishing colour and with a heroine (Alida Valli) admittedly and magnificently modelled on the Countess Sanseverina. By now his formal pre-occupations had become more apparent; and in *White Nights*, an adaptation from Dostoyevsky, a mannered melancholy, a romanticism of snow and mist and moony encounters on canal bridges, took command. Disconcerted admirers of the director coined a new phrase: this essay in fatalism, we were told, was 'neo-romanticism'.

When, in 1960, Visconti came to make *Rocco and his Brothers*, all the critical drums were beaten. Again, the history of a family, this time emigrants from the south to industrial Milan; again, a study in disintegration, this time through the corrupting forces of success and the city. Visconti's sheer power as a director, his magnetic pull on the audience, had never been more in evidence. Where *La Terra Trema* plots a remorseless chart of cause and effect, however, *Rocco* runs wild. The two boxer brothers, both in love with the same girl; the handing back of the girl by the saintly Rocco to the brother who has raped her; the savage, ritualistic murder and the final wild grief of the stricken family – this whole narrative gave full play to Visconti's instinct for excess, to that taste for grand opera apparent also in *Ossessione* and *La Terra Trema* but here barely kept in check by the disciplinary tug of fact. *Rocco* is a kind of souped-up neo-realism, owing part at least of its tension to the obvious clash between the lure of the decadent and the counter-impulse to construct a sweeping social panorama of our times.

Aristocrat by birth and Marxist by conviction, equally at

home in the cinema and the theatre, at Covent Garden or on location in a Sicilian fishing village, Visconti goes his own way: the director of one of the cinema's great realist films, and yet a film-maker who seems, in the long run, to stand apart from neo-realism. Other directors from the early days of the movement have pursued still more erratic courses. Rossellini, for more than a decade, has looked like an intelligent man in search of a subject. He has filmed a life of St Francis, a picture (*Europa 51*) in which Ingrid Bergman was called on to take the weight of the world on her shoulders, gone off to film in India, come back to a war subject (*Il Generale della Rovere*, with de Sica as an opportunist turned hero), reverted to the past with a Stendhal adaptation, then gone back yet again to the war years. Renato Castellani made two neo-realist comedies (*Due Soldi di Speranza* and *È Primavera*) ablaze with exuberance and affection, and has managed nothing since to equal them. Directors such as Luciano Emmer (*Sunday in August*) and Alberto Lattuada (*The Mill on the Po*) have never quite sustained the promise of their early films. Even the confident Federico Fellini, whose *I Vitelloni* set a world fashion for studies of drifting young men in glum provincial towns, and whose *La Strada* gave a realistic theme the kind of mystical overtones that would later be called Bergmanesque, seemed towards the late fifties somewhat to falter.

As has happened so often in the history of the cinema, the essentially collective art, a group of artists produced their best work simultaneously. Neo-realism had grown out of a particular historical moment: the sense of freedom and possibility and confident morning which followed the liberation of Rome; the sense of opportunity, and at the same time of deep social injustice. After the immediate post-war films (*Open City, Paisà*), the neo-realist directors took for their themes poverty and economic exploitation. Although the subjects themselves – as Zavattini said – were inexhaustible, once *La Terra Trema* and

Bicycle Thieves and *Umberto D* had presented their statements the film-makers concerned seemed unable to go further.

They had, in any case, little help or encouragement. Neorealism was to some extent a revolutionary cinema in a non-revolutionary society, as a statement of Zavattini's about *Miracle in Milan* makes sufficiently plain. 'The humble ones have no tanks,' he said, 'or they would have been ready to defend themselves.' But the humble ones rejected the austere logic of *La Terra Trema*. The Italy of Fiat and Olivetti, of the post-war economic miracle, the Italy of expanding trade and high fashion, was no less valid than Zavattini's world of the dispossessed. And in this new Italy the cinema played a leading part, with Hollywood productions moving in to Cinecittà, the big Rome studios, and Italian stars touring the world. The Italian studios reverted to the tradition of spectacle films, which had served them so well since the earliest days of the cinema. With a little assistance from abroad – Steve Reeves to play Hercules, Belinda Lee as Messalina – they again sent the gladiators out into the arena and delivered the Christians to the lions. The Via Veneto had taken over from Sunset Boulevard; Italian cinema was commercially buoyant; and if, by the late fifties, it seemed that much of the creative impulse had been exhausted, this again was nothing new in an art in which periods of high endeavour usually seem to be short-lived.

But Italy, meanwhile, had found a film-maker who was to speak for the sixties as unmistakably as de Sica and Rossellini had spoken for the forties. Michelangelo Antonioni had directed five features (only two of them at that time shown in Britain) before, at the 1960 Cannes Festival, his *L'Avventura* received its sensational screening. From the half-way mark, the showing of the film proceeded against a barrage of laughter and noisy dissent – a storm only equalled by the anger of the critics, who next day got together to sign a protest against the film's reception. Continental festival audiences notoriously enjoy shouting back at the screen; but Antonioni, emerging despondent and shaken from this ordeal, could hardly have imagined that within a year he would have become the most fashionable film-maker in Europe. *L'Avventura*, in any case, was not an isolated film. Antonioni had begun his career as a film journalist, like so many of his Italian colleagues, had gone to France during the war as assistant to Marcel Carné on *Les Visiteurs du Soir*, and had later directed several documentaries. When he made his first feature, *Cronaca di un Amore*, in 1950, he was already thirty-seven. Unlike most film-makers, who have to take their assignments as they come, his career since then has been pursued with a novelist's consistency of style and purpose.

In this first feature, *Cronaca di un Amore*, a couple are brought together and then pulled apart by a shared, irrational guilt. In *La Signora senza Camelie* a girl ventures forlornly into the world of the movies, the small-time splendours of a starlet's career. In *Le Amiche* a group of women living in Turin is put under the microscope; and the film develops as an acute study in boredom, restlessness, the futilities and agonies of purposeless living. *L'Avventura* again takes up the theme of betrayal: Sandro, the architect, has betrayed the career he might have had; Claudia, in her love for him, betrays her lost friend Anna; Sandro betrays Claudia. From these impossible relationships – although at the end of *L'Avventura* Sandro and Claudia come together in what Antonioni calls 'a kind of shared pity' – he moved in *La Notte* to a concentrated study of a marriage at the point of crisis. In the sixteen hours or so which the film's action covers, layers of pretence and illusion are stripped away from the central characters, a successful young novelist and his wife, until they confront each other in the cold dawn after an all-night party. And in *The Eclipse* this analysis of the sentiments (in Antonioni's phrase) is taken up once more as the Antonioni heroine, the girl open to experience, is confronted by those substitutes for the real thing which are all society seems to offer her. 'We don't have to know each other to love,' says the heroine, 'and perhaps we don't have to love. . . .' The eclipse of the emotions casts its shadow, and when darkness finally descends on a street corner it is as though a world were ending.

These recurring themes – the impermanence of love, the difficulty of communication, the ease of betrayal, of oneself or someone else – preoccupy Antonioni almost to the point of obsession. Men are 'sick of love', he has said, and there must be some advance in moral and emotional attitudes comparable to our advances in technology. We live in a world in which private life and public conventions are out of step, in which traditional moralities (and Antonioni, it ought to be remembered, is working in a country which still does not sanction divorce) bear increasingly little relation to the way people actually behave. The sickness he diagnoses is one that attacks people with time on their hands; and when, in *I Vinti* and *Il Grido*, he has moved outside his accustomed world, he has also made his least successful films. Antonioni's most typical characters are articulate, aware of their own situation, and all too conscious of how little help this intelligence is to them; for they are also victims of emotional fatigue, *la noia*, the secret urges to self-destruction. They are – like Antonioni himself – north Italians, so that in *L'Avventura* they come to Sicily as to a foreign country. Like Scott Fitzgerald, a writer whom he greatly admires, Antonioni's attitudes towards the society he confronts in his work are ambivalent, with the result that a strong creative tension is set up. The moralist may despise privilege without responsibility; the observer admits the lure even of a corrupting beauty.

Antonioni's themes are familiar enough: breakdown of communication has become the catchword of the age. But clichés only turn into clichés when they are treated as such. Antonioni's work acquires at least part of its validity from the fact that he really is a modern artist, a man daunted by our society but not at a fundamental level afraid of it. When he shows us

31

people dwarfed by the steel and concrete towers of Milan, he is not suggesting that the way to restore a sense of proportion is to pull down the buildings. Filming almost always on location – the mist-drenched Po Valley in *Il Grido*, the baroque towns and sun-scorched villages of Sicily in *L'Avventura*, Milan's plate-glass palaces in *La Notte*, the aggressively modern Roman suburb of *The Eclipse* – he sets up a tension between setting and characters, so that what happens seems to be in part conditioned by where it happens. The island search in *L'Avventura*, one of the most brilliantly sustained passages in the whole of modern cinema, gives us his technique at full stretch. Every encounter, every shot of rock and sea and barren terrain, every oblique, edged fragment of dialogue, every intrusion from without (the police launches, the helicopter) pushes forward this exploration of the landscape of the mind. 'I need to follow my characters beyond the moments conventionally considered important,' he has said, 'to show them even when everything appears to have been said.' But he also follows people in places, with that awareness of a setting which is one of the attributes of almost all the really great film-makers.

Antonioni's cast of mind is a novelist's, and his achievement has been to evolve a cinematic style equal to the pressure he wants to put on it, so that the dazzlingly involved and complex sentences he constructs with the camera hold together as solidly as words on the page. The look of his films – the bleakness and the beauty, the over-the-shoulder conversations, the camera style – can be copied, and has been. Every year the Italian cinema acquires new directors (Franco Rossi, Francesco Rosi, Elio Petri, Mauro Bolognini, Giuseppe Patroni Griffi are only a few of those who have emerged during recent years); and some of them have not much more to offer than a devoted pastiche of the master's manner. Fellini, too, has his imitators. *La Dolce Vita*, that elaborate fresco of modern Rome, with its brilliance and its vulgarity, its assured sense of how to move people about on the screen and its facile symbolism (a helicopter-borne statue of Christ to begin with; a dead fish on a dawn beach to end), set its own fashions, as it added a new phrase to the international gossip columnists' vocabulary. It is an ironic final postscript to neo-realism, too, that where the film-makers, ten years before, had taken their actors from the streets, Fellini now had the Roman aristocracy queueing for parts in this film which was supposedly to rip their world apart.

Part of the strength of the Italian cinema, however, derives from the fact that it cannot live down the neo-realist tradition, and probably would not if it could. Two of its newer directors, Pier Paolo Pasolini, the left-wing writer, and Ermanno Olmi, a young documentary film-maker, both chose to make feature films with entirely non-professional casts, to go out again into the crowded streets. Pasolini's *Accattone* made a jagged, searing comment from within on what it means to live beyond the law in Rome. Olmi's *Il Posto* brought a rueful, diffident, and enchanting humour, an undertow of gentle melancholy, to its account of a young office-boy with the prison walls of his first job closing in around him. These film-makers have almost nothing in common except the inheritance they are able so rewardingly to draw on, the neo-realist conscience.

To the outsider, the Italian cinema often looks chaotic. Too many films are made, and experts are always predicting economic catastrophe; censorship battles break out over controversial new productions; scripts are still put together on that Italian committee system whereby half a dozen writers are regularly engaged on a picture. Rome itself has become a headquarters for the cinema's floating population, the international camp-followers of the industry. But this cinema continues to live, not unprofitably, with its own confusions. The transition from *Bicycle Thieves* to *La Notte*, from the immediate social protest of neo-realism to the film which cuts out a slice of experience, leaving us to make up our own minds about what the screen shows us, sums up a good deal of the cinema history of the past fifteen years. When Antonioni said that if he had made *Bicycle Thieves*, he would have told us more about the man and less about the bicycle, he was speaking in terms that most of his colleagues would probably agree with. De Sica and Zavattini worked through statements, while the film directors of the sixties think rather in terms of questions. And this applies not only to Antonioni but to a film in the direct line of descent from neo-realism, Francesco Rosi's *Salvatore Giuliano*. This intensely political film, an account of a divided Sicily in which a bandit could become an uncrowned king, repeatedly puts questions to which history has as yet failed to provide an answer; and does so with an objectivity which assumes an unusually sophisticated response in its audience. But the foundation in realist intention remains: the Italians never allow us to forget for long that their modern cinema began with a social conscience. The value of the inheritance has been proved over and over again.

3. Which Picture Made the Money?

'Neo-realism' has been one of the convenient portmanteau words (and why 'neo', in any case, some critics have asked?), but inevitably the pursuit of realism goes back in cinema history almost as far as you care to travel – to Renoir's *Toni*, made in 1934, to the Germans a little earlier, to Flaherty's *Nanook* and Dziga-Vertov's kino-eye, to Lumière's train. Film-making did not begin in a studio: it moved there for convenience and is always ready to move out again. Distinctions between the documentary, or film of fact, and the fiction work have not always been entirely clear. One thing the Italians did was to make them even less so, to smudge the boundary lines between the imagined and the actual: *La Terra Trema*, which really has very little to do with documentary, was described as such by at least one English reviewer. The breaking down of the barriers which would keep all the fact on one side of the fence and all the fiction on the other exerts an abiding influence.

But the influence has been more pervasive than direct: no one in a film *industry* was going to copy pictures which, however cheaply made, had shown almost no capacity for earning money. Neo-realism shook up a few established ideas; it reminded people of what could be managed on derisively small budgets;

it left some film-makers dissatisfied with the kind of things they were doing. And it coincided, as far as the British and American cinemas were concerned, with the impetus to a greater realism which had stirred in both industries during the war and was certainly not dead at the end of it. In Britain the documentary tradition of the thirties had come into its own, with the work of Humphrey Jennings, pre-eminently the cinema's poet of the blitz and the home front, the factual records such as *Desert Victory*, and the features like Pat Jackson's *Western Approaches* or Carol Reed's *The Way Ahead*. For America, films such as Frank Capra's *Why We Fight* series or John Huston's *San Pietro* performed the same service, as information or propaganda or straight record.

Artists who had gone to war might be expected to want to record their experiences, to come back in the mood for a moral stock-taking. A film studio can be one of the world's more insulated places, and the war released a good deal of under-used energy. But the popular cinema had also acquired a certain split personality: realism-plus-propaganda on the one hand; entertainment of the blandest and most relaxing kind on the other. Betty Grable reigned; even Bette Davis turned up in an all-star musical to sing 'They're either too young or too old' for the awe-struck soldiery. The end of the war killed off such stand-bys as the Occupied Europe adventure, the home-front film, the Hollywood Canteen musical. New formulas had to be devised, and the question was how far they would accommodate such impulses towards realism as were clearly present. America found one answer and Britain another; answers determined not only by the attitudes of the national industries, but also, it seems clear in retrospect, by the different degrees of post-war fatigue.

The British answer came swiftly: the harsher realities and immediacies were out, and the film-makers went back to the studios. To a formidable extent, by comparison with any other country, our cinema has been (and for that matter remains) one of literary adaptation. Where French or Italian film-makers are as likely as not to begin with a script or an idea, ours start with a novel or a play. And the British critic, until fairly recently, has often enough looked at the result in terms of truth to the text rather than truth to the film, so that the more irrefutable a film's literary credentials the more chance it has stood of finding favour. So, after the war, the literary tradition continued. Anthony Asquith filmed Rattigan plays (*The Winslow Boy*, *The Browning Version*), David Lean filmed Dickens (*Great Expectations*, *Oliver Twist*), Thorold Dickinson made the elegant and atmospheric *Queen of Spades* (from Pushkin), Laurence Olivier's *Hamlet* followed his wartime *Henry V*, Carol Reed made *Odd Man Out* (from F. L. Green) and *The Fallen Idol* (from Graham Greene).

David Lean and Carol Reed, both technicians' directors, the kind of film-makers consistently respected by other professionals for the calibre of their craftsmanship, led the field. Lean's *Brief Encounter*, greatly enjoyed by the French because it confirmed so many theories about the cold and conscience-stricken British, had put an England of glum suburban tea-rooms and windswept railway platforms on to the screen. The film, although it wears none too well, has that particular cinematic trick of summing up a mood and a moment: Noël Coward and Rachmaninov and Celia Johnson; tea and toast and the mute despair of station waiting-rooms. Lean's *Great Expectations* had grace and intelligence and a fine narrative control – as well as a flashing little performance by Alec Guinness which in memory outstays many of his star parts. Carol Reed shot at a rather higher target in *Odd Man Out*, the story of a wounded man on the run through the streets of Belfast, with the night closing in on him, the city a garish assortment of potential betrayers and rescuers. In this uneven film, and more consistently in *The Third Man* (1949), Reed let us see the full creative strength of his hand, as he has done only intermittently since. The dark and corrupt Vienna of *The Third Man*, with its raw nerves and dilapidated splendours, brought out all his edged talent for applying atmospheric pressure. Harry Lime, joint creation of Reed, Orson Welles, and Graham Greene, walked straight into the cinema's mythology on the strength of a line of dialogue about Switzerland and cuckoo clocks and a shot of a hand clutching at a sewer grating. Reed himself has never found a better setting for a movie.

In both these films, as in *The Fallen Idol* and *Outcast of the Islands*, Reed took for his central characters men at odds with the world and themselves, half-heroes, fugitives by necessity or by choice, begetters of violence. But this director has never encouraged critics anxious to trace themes running through his work. Interrogated as an artist he has preferred to answer as a craftsman, with that characteristically English suspicion of the pretentious which would prefer us to think that anything we notice which looks like a statement could only have got there by chance. Reviewing *The Third Man*, Richard Winnington had a perceptive comment about its creator:

Probably the most brilliant craftsman of the modern cinema, yet one who is devoid of the urges that make a really great director. Sensitive and humane and dedicated, he would seem to be enclosed from life, with no specially strong feelings about the stories that come his way to film other than that they should be something he can perfect and polish with a craftsman's love.

Reticence, good taste, a feeling that the proper job for a film director is to interpret rather than to create, to stick to his brief (the script) rather than to stand up and declaim on his own account: these attitudes characterized the British cinema. Overwhelming creative pressures, of the kind which lead an artist to insist that he will make this film and none other, were missing — as, indeed, they still largely seem to be. When Ealing Studios, that tight little nursery of all the talents under the headmastership of Sir Michael Balcon, instituted its famous series of comedies, a pattern formed. Ealing trained at least two major directors, in the cool, francophile Robert Hamer (*Kind Hearts and Coronets, Father Brown*) and the more volatile and wider-ranging Alexander Mackendrick (*Whisky Galore, The Lady-killers, Sweet Smell of Success*). Its most characteristic comedies celebrated an England enclosed and sheltered, a Winnie-the-Pooh land based on Ealing Green. Isolated communities – like the inhabitants of Pimlico, setting up their independent state in the teeth of Whitehall – delighted in gestures of anti-bureaucratic defiance; old trains, old steamers were cherished, ramshackle machinery coaxed into life; the mildest, most genial, and least competent of law-breakers were adopted as Ealing's heroes. 'Post office is closed,' chirped its guardian, Joan Greenwood, in *Whisky Galore*, when authority attempted to assert itself. The grace and humour – which were considerable – ensure the survival of the best of these films; but the problem Ealing could never solve was how to break loose from its own formulas, how to avoid the impression of an inbred tradition.

If Ealing's cinema at its most characteristic looks in retrospect like an amalgam of *The Times* Fourth Leaders, the London-to-Brighton car race, and the village cricket match, it co-existed with another brand of film-making summed up (for those who can bring themselves to remember the films at all) in the smile of the Gainsborough Lady. If this trademark seemed to acquire, as the years went by, a suggestion of ineffable condescension, no doubt commercial success offered some justification. Escapism in the British cinema, during the war and after, involved endless permutations of the same star équipe, as James Mason and Stewart Granger, Margaret Lockwood and Phyllis Calvert, flung themselves into Regency disguise, took to the roads as highwaywomen, poisoned off old retainers (with, if memory can be trusted, doses from large bottles obligingly labelled 'poison'), and cheated each other out of inheritances. Dennis Price as Byron; Stewart Granger as Paganini; two luckless British starlets injudiciously required to lay about each other with whips in the Bois de Boulogne – film after film offered this kitchen-maid escapism. Gainsborough flogged its galloping tosh horse; Ealing had its pack of jokers; Michael Powell (in *The Red Shoes*) harnessed ballet to fantasy. One way and another, this was a cinema for a society weary of restrictions and ration-books; and it seems more than mere coincidence that it barely survived the end of rationing.

During these years, in any case, British cinema had run into one of those financial crises which have periodically dogged its progress, affecting its artists as well as its businessmen. In the first post-war years the industry's mood was euphoric: production was stepped up from twenty-eight first features in 1945 to sixty-three in 1948, and the Rank Group, responsible on its own account for half the 1948 total, had decided that it ought to be possible to break into the American market. This enterprise failed, as the American film historian Richard Griffith wrote in *Sight and Sound*, because 'it was clear that Mr Rank's big films could not achieve sufficient bookings [in the United States] to justify the costs which mass distribution entails'. However well British films might go down in the specialized cinemas of New York and other big cities, this richest of mass markets could not be prised open. And a few very expensive ventures – Gabriel Pascal's *Caesar and Cleopatra*, or *London Town* (devised to launch Sid Field as a screen comedian) – were to hang, embarrassing albatrosses, round the neck of the industry which had risked them, and in doing so over-extended its resources.

In 1947, in an attempt to meet the balance of payments problem, the British Government imposed a heavy import duty on American films. The American industry promptly retaliated with an embargo on film shipments to Britain which lasted for eight months.

A gloom of uncertainty settled over the whole industry [to quote the P.E.P. Report on the British Film Industry]. ... They seemed to have lost their main competitor at a single blow and to have been presented with an opportunity to dominate their home market. It was a challenge which they could not ignore. But ... it was a challenge beyond the bounds of economic possibility.

The Rank Group tried to meet it; but as Lord (then Mr) Rank had to inform his shareholders:

Many of the films we produced were not of a quality to ensure even reasonable returns. ... Our plans to meet an unexpected and critical situation were too ambitious.

Rank, an organization so large that it effectively dominated the industry, had to declare losses on production amounting to well over £3,000,000.

This was the climate of despondency in which the Government stepped in to assist production, largely through the setting up in 1949 of the National Film Finance Corporation, to act as a government film bank by advancing loans to independent producers. Then came the 'Eady Plan' (so called after its originator, the late Sir Wilfred Eady), and the establishment of the British Film Production Fund, to channel a percentage of the box-office earnings directly back to the producers. These forms of aid to production still survive; as indeed the P.E.P. Report, published in 1952, had forecast that they were bound to do.

If the public considers it desirable for political, cultural, or economic reasons that British films should be produced [the Report concluded], then it must be prepared for the Government not only to protect the industry indefinitely, but also to aid it financially for as far ahead as can be seen.

The crisis and its ramifications, such as the £3,000,000 loan made by the National Film Finance Corporation to keep British Lion, Sir Alexander Korda's company, on its feet, and the eventual take-over of the company in the public interest, or the falling off in employment in the industry between 1948 and 1950, produced an atmosphere of enervating timidity. In addition, the audience decline had already begun: 1946's thirty-one million a week had become 1951's twenty-six million, so that in retrospect, enormous as this figure looks by comparison with the present audience statistics, the industry's *crise de nerfs* seems justified. After the vaunting ambitions of the first post-war years and the dreams of glory in the American market came the cautious fifties. But caution, for too many creative talents, also meant a kind of stagnation. Of those bright hopes of fifteen or so years ago, the Ealing group, the post-war innovators, how many – or how few – survive in a really creative sense in the British cinema of the sixties? How many film-makers have been idle for long periods, or have left the industry, or have chosen (as David Lean did with *The Bridge on the River Kwai* and *Lawrence of Arabia*) to work for American impresarios on a scale which the British industry cannot permit them? A Government Working Party, which published its findings in 1949, had found that 'extravagance in the British film industry was allowed to go beyond all reasonable bounds'. The reckoning brought with it a caution not merely financial, a fear of imaginative as well as commercial extravagance, a rejection of risk, a policy which left the artist all too little room to manoeuvre while the accountants worked at balancing the books. Ealing Studios vanished in 1956, swallowed up in an uncomfortably symbolic transition into the B.B.C.'s television empire; Gainsborough had gone years before, as had the Rank Organization's luckless Charm School. The post-war foundations had not been quite solid enough, and the traumatic effects of the 1948 crisis lingered on.

In 1947 the British market brought in $68,000,000 to the American film industry, or approximately a quarter of its net income. The most valuable of Hollywood's overseas markets, Britain was also – and remains – the most accessible and the most open to influence. In economic terms, Hollywood's domination of world cinema has been as simple as it has been inevitable: the home audience (estimated at just on ninety million a week in the first post-war year) gave an unbeatable lead, since the only other countries with comparable populations (India, say, with its own huge industry) were content or compelled to produce work almost entirely for home consumption. Foreign films had only a precarious foothold in the American market, while in Europe governments had found it necessary to impose quotas to ensure that a reasonable percentage of screen time went to the national product. The whole system of film distribution, in fact, depended on a steady flow of product to the cinemas such as only Hollywood could supply; and an industry cut off from Hollywood was an industry in trouble, as the British cinema discovered. Confident that it held all the aces, the American industry could play its commercial hand more or less as it pleased. Hollywood's grip could be loosened in only one way: by the American industry's own decision to cut production, so that cinemas in the United States would more readily take foreign-made films and a larger share of the European market would be left to indigenous industries. This, in effect, is what has happened during the last decade. In 1950, for instance, two-thirds of the Italian box-office takings went to American films, and less than a quarter to Italy's own films; by 1960 the American share had dropped to forty-one per cent, the Italian had risen to forty-five per cent.

In the mid forties, however, all these developments remained unthinkable. If anyone in Hollywood had any suspicion that within a decade the home audience would be cut in half, certainly he never let on. This was an entertainment industry with the firmest of all assets: an automatic, unquestioning, unshakeable audience. If a film did badly at the box-office, there was always another one behind it on the assembly line; if the public stayed away one week, they would be back the next.

The American directors returned from the war with ambitions to be satisfied. Some of them joined together to form their own companies, rather than accept the disciplines of the studios. Films such as John Ford's *They Were Expendable* or Lewis Milestone's *A Walk in the Sun*, two poetic records of Americans in action, came as personal responses to war from men who had grown up with the cinema. Another veteran, William Wyler, set out to make, in *The Best Years of Our Lives*, a study of the newly demobilized ex-serviceman, a gesture to the American way of life and the American dream. Produced by Sam Goldwyn, written by Robert Sherwood, and photographed (memorably) by Gregg Toland, *The Best Years of Our Lives* stands as a memorial to a certain tradition of showmanship, in which commercial confidence, technical command, homely good sense, sentimental over-statement, *naïveté*, and sophistication all come together. It is one of those films in which nuggets of truth and toughness lurk for the finding, moments of a specifically Hollywood inspiration breaking through all the hot chocolate sauce which is also quintessential Hollywood.

Side-stepped by the British cinema, realism was promptly and intelligently commercialized by the Americans. The new thing in the cinema, in these years, became the location-made thriller (Jules Dassin's *The Naked City*, Henry Hathaway's *Call Northside 777*, Elia Kazan's *Boomerang*), and the problem picture which overlapped it (Edward Dmytryk's *Crossfire*, Kazan's *Gentleman's Agreement*, Clarence Brown's *Intruder in the Dust*). Location shooting has become so much a matter of course everywhere that one forgets just how rarely Hollywood had bothered to go out and find a real city street, when the one on the back lot was always ready to hand. A thriller like *The Naked City*, produced by Mark Hellinger, a newspaperman turned film-maker, had the on-its-toes look of live reporting:

no more, but certainly no less. Soon enough, inevitably, this whole trend ran itself into the ground. Film after film announced that its material came straight from the files of such-and-such a police department. Chases round the sewers and up and down tenement stairs; questioning of sleazy suspects by hard-eyed detectives; spoken narratives introduced by a date, a place, a time; the wail of police sirens and the thud of running feet on pavements – these were fine while the impulse stayed fresh, but the moment came when all that remained was to turn the whole thing over to television and 'Dragnet'.

The problem picture, meanwhile, turned out in effect to mean a series of pleas for tolerance for America's racial minorities. Here was Hollywood pinning its social conscience to its sleeve, self-critical, as the American cinema has always been, genuinely concerned, but still careful that nothing too taxing should be required of its audience. Characteristic protagonists were a journalist pretending to be a Jew, so that Gregory Peck could encounter race prejudice; a coloured family endeavouring to pass as white (and so played by white actors); a coloured girl (in *Pinky*) white enough to be played by Jeanne Crain. Much more recently *A Majority of One*, which set Alec Guinness's Japanese millionaire against Rosalind Russell's Brooklyn Jewess, found Hollywood still playing the immemorial game: the dialogue can be as high-minded as it pleases, and the audience can take it in its stride, for toleration of an Alec Guinness or a Gregory Peck imposes no strain. Perhaps the most ironic comment on this whole grimly well-meaning cycle of films came from the playwright Moss Hart, scriptwriter of *Gentleman's Agreement*. A studio workman, he said, told him that he'd learnt a lot while they were making the film. Flattered, Hart pressed for details. 'Well,' said the convert, 'I'll know never to be rude to a Jew again, because it may turn out that he's really a Gentile.'

Crossfire (in which, another sign of the times, the murder victim became a Jew instead of, as in Richard Brooks's original novel, a homosexual) had a hard edge of violence, accepted and assimilated, which made it better value than the more well-mannered brand of problem picture. And in fact the open melo-drama, from the wartime *Double Indemnity*, which virtually set a cycle in motion, through *Mildred Pierce*, with Joan Crawford in suffering close-up against the night sky, to such rococo exercises as *The Strange Love of Martha Ivers*, has proved a good deal more durable than many of the movies which set out to be significant at all costs, and ended up looking merely laborious. Hollywood was still filming for an American public, which meant that it had not yet become self-conscious about the way movies accepted violence as a norm. James Agee, the best American critic of the period, and one of the best writers about the cinema in any period, summed up something of the whisky-and-cigarette-smoke flavour of such movies in his review of Robert Rossen's *Body and Soul*, a film which, like *The Set-Up*, shook new life into the jaded theme of corruption in the prize-ring.

. . . There is quick, satirical observation, a sense of meanness to match the meanness of the world they are showing, a correct assumption of cynical knowledge in the audience which relieves them of the now almost universal practice of drawing diagrams for the retarded, and a general quality of tension and pleasure in good craftsmanship.

Agee went on to complain that this craftsmanship, so strong in the Hollywood of the thirties, had to be looked for and cherished in the post-war American film. The critic who began his film-going in the war years, looking back now from the perspective of the sixties, would probably speak in exactly the same terms. Is this a comment on the critics, or on Hollywood? In any event, a look at the movies made or released in an average year (1948) displays a range of talent at work which could hardly be equalled today. Comedy: Preston Sturges (*Unfaithfully Yours*),

Billy Wilder (*A Foreign Affair*), Frank Capra (*State of the Union*). Melodrama: Alfred Hitchcock (not at his best, by a long way, with *Rope* and the dreary experiment of the ten-minute take), John Farrow (*The Big Clock*), Jules Dassin (*The Naked City*). Musicals: Vincente Minnelli (*The Pirate*), Rouben Mamoulian (*Summer Holiday*), Charles Walters (*Easter Parade*). Westerns: John Ford (*Fort Apache*) and Howard Hawks (*Red River*). Sentiment: George Stevens (*I Remember Mama*) and, idiosyncratically, Max Ophuls, whose *Letter from an Unknown Woman* must be one of the most evocatively 'European' pictures ever made in Hollywood. Post-war problem: Fred Zinnemann's *The Search*. Add one film which only came out of Hollywood by a fluke, Orson Welles's *Macbeth*, one which had nothing whatsoever to do with Hollywood, Robert Flaherty's *Louisiana Story*, and one dry and bouncy little comedy, *So This is New York*, which set the new company formed by Stanley Kramer and Carl Foreman on its way, and one still has only a selective list of films, most of which would stand reseeing – and not only on television.

Most of these films had major studios behind them, with everything that meant in terms of trademark: Metro gave its musicals 'the M.G.M. sound', Fox went in for a very clean black-and-white camerawork, and so on. The frustrations of working inside Hollywood's big studio system have been exhaustively chronicled, in the novels in which so many screenwriters have tried to work off their disillusionment, or in a book such as Lillian Ross's *Picture*, which documents every stage in the making of John Huston's *The Red Badge of Courage*. Miss Ross quoted one of the executives of M.G.M.:

'I don't care too much what kind of pictures we make. When a picture is liked in this office, it is liked everywhere . . . All of us here like the kind of pictures that do well at the box-office.'

She quoted Louis B. Mayer:

'We had two pictures here. An Andy Hardy picture, with little Mickey Rooney, and *Ninotchka*, with Greta Garbo. *Ninotchka* got the prizes. Blue ribbons! Purple ribbons! . . . Which picture made the money? Andy Hardy made the money. Why? Because it won praise from the heart. No ribbons.'

So sounded the voice of the old, confident Hollywood, speaking out of all the accumulated lessons of the box-office. But at the same time the big studios recognized their own dependence on talent; and, with their stable market and controlled production costs, could take a number of calculated chances. If there was no place, finally, for the complete individualist – for Chaplin, who in 1947 had made *Monsieur Verdoux* and seen it subjected to ferocious attack, or for Welles, who worked under increasing pressure – the system still needed and assimilated almost any talent which could manage to live with it. Other national cinemas have fluctuated according to the ability, determination, or commercial opportunism of the people working in them at any given time. Only Hollywood seemed able to go on for ever, sucking in talent and ideas like some mammoth vacuum cleaner, converting the stylistic innovation of one year into the common currency of the next, an indestructible symbol of everything that goes to make up mass entertainment.

Yet this Hollywood died, one might almost say, with Louis B. Mayer. Its foundation had been confidence; the kind of commercial arrogance which could say – and believe, and have authority for believing – that 'all of us here like the kind of pictures that do well at the box-office'. A system had been built on this certainty, on the ability to take boys out of garages and girls from behind soda-fountains and convert them into international currency, the stars who walked through the dreams of the world. This confidence had grown up with the cinema since its fairground beginnings; and when it went, it was as though the big top had fallen in. For ten years or more, the ringmasters have been struggling to get it up again.

4. The Nervous Years

The combination of symbolic and news values, cherished by Hollywood in its good times, becomes a liability whenever anything goes wrong. Exposed and vulnerable, Hollywood is a perpetual target, badgered by the Legion of Decency, harried by women's organizations, forced to listen to pressure-groups which insist that some aspect of national life is not getting a fair deal on the screen. However cranky the complaint, whether it has to do with an actress's private life or a writer's political affiliations, or the fact that a film (like *Death of a Salesman*) has shown a profession as unattractive, Hollywood cannot afford to ignore these voices from the audience. In 1947, however, the really big attack was launched, and official Hollywood closed its ranks in fear against an assault which was largely motivated by fear. On 18 October 1947 Representative J. Parnell Thomas, chairman of the House Committee on un-American Activities, assembled his committee in Washington to conduct 'an investigation of Communism in motion pictures'. When the hearings broke up, a fortnight later, thirty-nine witnesses had been called, including 'ten prominent figures in Hollywood whom the Committee had evidence were members of the Communist Party'. These witnesses, who openly defied the Committee's authority ('I am not on trial here . . . this Committee is on trial here before the American people,' said one of them), were the famous 'Hollywood Ten'.

These 1947 hearings produced moments of high and desperate comedy, when such impeccably respectable producers as Jack Warner and Louis B. Mayer were called on to justify the pro-Soviet films they had made during the war; when Adolphe Menjou, a 'friendly' witness, testified out of his 'particular study of Marxism, Fabian Socialism, Communism, Stalinism, and its probable effects on the American people if they ever gain power here'; when Mrs Rogers, mother of Ginger Rogers, explained that she had dissuaded her daughter from playing in *Sister Carrie* because it was 'open propaganda'. One of the last witnesses called to testify was Bertolt Brecht, who asserted that he had never joined the Party and won an unexpected compliment from Mr Thomas: 'He is doing all right. He is doing much better than many other witnesses you have brought here.'

But the comedy remained occasional and incidental, an ironic footnote to a fortnight which itself proved no more than a presage of the McCarthyist years. The Hollywood Ten were given prison sentences for contempt of Congress; and the Association of Motion Picture Producers came out with the announcement that, 'Their actions have been a disservice to their employers and have impaired their usefulness to the industry.' No member of the Ten, the Association said, would be employed again 'until such time as he has purged himself of contempt and declares under oath that he is not a Communist'. So, under pressure and protest, Hollywood instituted the beginnings of a blacklist, which was to spread out in wider and wider circles from this original nucleus. By the time another big round of hearings had ended, in 1951, approximately two hundred people, about half of them writers, many of them individuals who had merely been 'named' to the Committee by cooperative witnesses, were no longer free to work in the American cinema.

Clearly, Hollywood had its Communists. Left-wing intellectuals whose social conscience had been roused during the fellow-travelling thirties, who had spoken at rallies for Spain and given money for strikers in California; actors whose progress from a tough East Side childhood to the Hollywood of conspicuous wealth had left them with a sense of guilt: such were the recruits, and the Party must have cherished and cosseted them. The true history of these years, including just what Hollywood Communism really meant, remains to be written. Self-evidently though, the extent of Communist influence on the actual content of films remained very trivial, even if, as one witness firmly argued, a line of dialogue such as 'share and share alike – that's democracy' yielded plain evidence of subversive intent. No one really thought that American movies were in danger of going Communist. No one really denies that what did the damage was the blacklist, the atmosphere of panicky tension, the fear of what names might be thrown around at the hearings, all the harassments and pressures of the years of suspicion.

As early as 1948, William Wyler was saying that he would not be permitted to make *The Best Years of Our Lives* in the new Hollywood. By 1953 Carl Foreman, scriptwriter of *The Men* and *High Noon*, and Joseph Losey, the director, were among the many who had moved to Europe. Even here, for several years, they could take no credit for the work they did in the cinema, so that two of Losey's features carry other men's names on their credits. Some of the writers kept busy, disposing of their work anonymously if not exactly in secret. 'The major studios,' said the blacklisted writer Dalton Trumbo in a magazine article, 'were openly in the black market [for scripts].' When, in 1956, a Mr Robert Rich could not be found to take the Academy Award due to him for a screen story called *The Brave One*, it eventually turned out, to official embarrassment, that Mr Rich sheltered the identity of the proscribed Mr Trumbo.

The whole business took a heavy toll not only in immediate human terms – the careers abruptly curtailed, the distinguished writers acting like secret agents in fixing up their hole-and-corner assignments, the families sent into virtual exile – but in Hollywood reactions. American films tended to become either very safe and cautious and respectable, or expressions, tinged with hysteria, of an underlying strain and uncertainty. Hollywood's radical conscience had been on trial; and the people who had represented it, if they were not among the exiles from the industry, had been sternly taught the language of conformism.

Meanwhile, a nervy industry had to fight for its audience. Attendance figures had begun their slow downhill slide in the late forties, the decline speeding up as soon as television became a real threat. By the middle fifties, audiences were down to half the 1946 figure, and as an inevitable consequence Hollywood cut back severely on production. In 1951 the studios' output was 369 features; by 1955 the figure was down to 241. At the same time, the American cinema became each year more dependent on its overseas markets, not just for extra profits but for basic revenue. As one writer in *Variety*, the trade paper, reported, 'Two-thirds of our pictures are failing to return their negative costs in the States and Canada.'

For a while, Hollywood hit back with schoolboy malice. Comedy heroes were always kicking in television screens; any TV set switched on during a film could be relied on to produce a wildly erratic picture. More seriously, the industry began to reconsider the shape and dimensions of its own screens. Primitive logic imposed its unassailable solution: the cinema had two actual advantages over television and one potential one in that its pictures were larger, many of them were in colour, and they might be three-dimensional. Consequently, these advantages must be fully exploited: larger screens, more colour, and 3–D movies became the new orthodoxy.

Cinerama came first: the initial programme *This is Cinerama* opened on Broadway in the autumn of 1952 and soon set off on its travels round the world. Here was an enormous curved screen – or, rather, a triptych of three screens – six times the size of the traditional cinema image. The frame opened out drastically; even if the joins between the three panels shook a little, the spectator not only got something very big to look at, but an illusion of depth and perspective. But Cinerama remains one of the technical advances with which it is very difficult to cope in other than circus terms: nobody really wants that much space to play with, except for battles and aeroplane trips and landscape panoramas; no one can do a great deal to concentrate attention when the screen itself takes so much mastering. Not very surprisingly, it took ten years after Cinerama's first opening before anyone chanced a fiction film in the process; though *How the West Was Won* may very well prove a portent for the future. If and when we watch films at home via Pay Television, with only a few cinemas surviving on their spectacular shows, Cinerama will undoubtedly be among them. But the cost of special equipment restricts it to the occasional big city cinema. It certainly could not solve the problems of 1952.

The stereoscopic fashion, also an offshoot of 1952, came and went so fast that it is difficult to remember just how seriously some people in the film industry were prepared to take it. A jungle adventure called *Bwana Devil*, shot in a process optimistically known as Natural Vision, made quite a bit of money as a novelty by offering its audience the appealing if illusory delight of 'a lion in your lap'. Quickly, some major studios decided to move into 3–D: Warners made *House of Wax*, a revamp of an old horror picture, throwing a few corpses stereoscopically around; Hitchcock's *Dial M for Murder* was shot in 3–D, though by the time the picture was finished the fashion had already ended and a flat version was shown. Audiences flinched under a hail of assegais, as pictures were rushed cheaply on to the screen to make the most of the passing fancy. Depth on the screen had been an illusion, achieved by deep-focus camera-work, perspective, and gradations of light, all of which drew the spectator into the image. 3-D pictures were chiefly concerned with the amount of assorted hardware they could project out of it. But people disliked having to wear the Polaroid spectacles necessary to bring the double image into correct focus; and, having once got them on, proved equally reluctant to give them up at the door of the cinema. Quietly, and very quickly, 3-D was dropped. No doubt it will come back, sooner or later, in an improved form. But the stereoscopic image, at least as we have experienced it, remains an unnatural one because of the opposition it sets up between background and foreground.

As befitted a major company, Twentieth Century-Fox moved altogether more sedately into CinemaScope, the first attempt to bring the big screen into the area of practical, everyday film-making. They took their time over *The Robe* (1953), linking their new screen system with the kind of expensive, heavy-weight religious epic which always goes well at the box-office. Where the traditional cinema screen had been a 4 × 3 rectangle, CinemaScope offered a 2·5:1 oblong. The people who devised the system went for the greatest possible width, considerations of height being governed by the actual architecture of cinemas: there is no point in a screen whose top will be effectively hidden from people at the back of the stalls by the overhang of the circle. As with sound, which had been a practical proposition long before Warners adopted it in an earlier period of commercial uncertainty, CinemaScope itself was nothing new. Its inventor, a French scientist named Henri Chrétien, had in fact demonstrated it, years before, to an uninterested industry which had hardly come to grips with the talkies. Now Fox bought it, renamed it (the original, and clumsier, title was Anamorphoscope), took the ageing Professor Chrétien on a barn-storming tour of demonstrations, and announced that the company's entire product would be in their new process. Its basis was an anamorphic lens, which enabled the wide-screen image to be squeezed into a conventional 35 mm. frame, with a compensating lens on the projector to expand it again. Although some cinemas (notably in Britain the Rank circuit) at first resisted the pressure to re-equip with the new screens and the stereophonic sound devices that went with them, Fox's all-or-nothing determination paid off handsomely.

As a bigger screen became everyone's ambition, cinema managers took to projecting everything in some kind of wide screen version, topping and tailing the pictures so that actors lost their feet, even their heads, as old-style 4×3 films were uneasily adjusted to the newer ratios. And, after CinemaScope, came the flood of wide-screen processes: Paramount's Vista-Vision, with an aspect ratio (width to height) of 1·85:1; the French Dyaliscope, the Japanese TohoScope; Todd–AO (named after Mike Todd), Panavision, Technirama, Super Technirama 70, and so on. The '70' in this last unwieldy title refers to the actual film, 70 mm. as opposed to the traditional 35 mm., so that the size of the frame is actually doubled. Screen sizes vary from the utilitarian wide screen of a back-street cinema to the expanses of the London Dominion or Coliseum; aspect ratios range from 1·66:1 (standard wide screen) to 2·5:1. In effect, every big-screen process is after the same end: the largest manageable screen image, with the minimum of distortion.

Very quickly indeed, these new screen shapes achieved acceptance. Jokes about CinemaScope's letter-box format, about the way actors in CinemaScope films always had to be shot lying down, complaints about huge, threatening close-ups with eyebrows twenty feet across, vanished into screen history. Jean Cocteau was sardonic – 'the next time I write a poem I'll use a big sheet of paper' – and Jean Renoir philosophic – 'our contemporaries see things horizontally; the previous generation saw things vertically. Neither you nor I can do anything to alter that.' More seriously, critics argued that the oblong was a less 'natural' shape for composition than the rectangle (as with painting and the 'golden mean', etc.), that it made it unnecessarily difficult to focus attention or to cut smoothly from one angle to another. In fact, the first CinemaScope films moved with limiting caution, their makers simply tending to photograph as much as it was possible to get on the screen. As soon as the artists got their hands on CinemaScope, however, the complaints mostly evaporated. The oblong *does* work for intimate scenes (anything from *A Star is Born* to *The Innocents*); it *does* work in black-and-white (anything from the Japanese *Conflagration* to the Italian *La Grande Guerra*); it *does* permit concentration.

Clearly CinemaScope would be a fairly meaningless shape for a cinema constructed on montage, or associational editing; the modern cinema, however, has not been moving that way, but rather towards a more open style of film-making which the wide screen, with its opportunities for composition in depth and width, for the sequence built on camera movement rather than on cutting, suits very well. Ideally, directors ought to be free to choose whatever screen process they prefer to work in for a given subject. In fact studios often leave no choice: if the film is to be made at all, it must be done in the system they favour. In general, though, the change in the proportions of the screen has amounted not to the artistic retreat, or artistic revolution, some people envisaged ten years ago, but simply to a technical innovation of undoubted value. Only a few real diehards would still challenge the very existence of the wide screen; just as only a few diehards, well into the thirties, were still bewailing the debasing effects of sound.

The very fact that the big-screen revolution was so complete meant that the cinema needed something more to attract its audience. If all the screens are larger, then size alone has lost its selling power. Hollywood tried, for a while, to make the kind of pictures it had been making for years, but to present them on bigger screens. Then, slowly, it adopted the policy of the so-called blockbuster, the films like *The Ten Commandments* and *Around the World in 80 Days* and *South Pacific*, which would settle down at some big cinema and run for months or years, films which cost millions to make and thousands to sell, the films which actually admitted that cinema-going was no longer a habit and acted accordingly.

Essentially, the blockbusters called for showmanship; the old-time deMille version with pop religion, orgies and uplift, or the three-ring circus Mike Todd variety. Producers had to study what would bring people into the cinemas and, no less important, what would keep them out. The Bible worked, as always; romantic travelogues worked, with acres of scenery and a theme-song intoned moonily over the credits; musicals worked, provided they originated in big stage successes. The essentially film musical, as Vincente Minnelli (*Meet Me in St Louis*, *An American in Paris*, *The Band Wagon*) and Gene Kelly and Stanley Donen (*On the Town*, *Singin' in the Rain*) had been lovingly developing it, was an early casualty. Such films had relied on dancing, colour, pace, the elegance or the drive of their visual style. Big screen musicals were slowed down, to look more like the original stage shows; song and dance began to count for less than 'production values' – the trappings of size. Musical stars (Judy Garland, Doris Day, Fred Astaire) turned straight actors; and straight actors (Deborah Kerr, Yul Brynner, Rosalind Russell) moved into the new musicals.

Unhappily for their makers, the biggest of the big films can scarcely hope to parallel the giants of the past, from *Intolerance* to *Gone With the Wind*. The sheer cost, in modern terms, of hiring extras and building sets on the old scale weighs against them. A 1960s *Intolerance* is just not a practical proposition – which is something to be thankful for. But even the block-buster, it seems, is losing its exclusiveness, that quality of a special attraction, a once-for-all thing in the cinema, which it started out with. At the end of 1962, eight out of the twenty-nine London cinemas which advertise in *The Times* were occupied by what are known to the film trade as 'hard ticket' shows, long-runners firmly dug in for the winter and ranging from *Lawrence of Arabia* to *How the West Was Won*. One way and another, the blockbuster policy has managed to make any Hollywood film running less than two hours look almost like a second feature.

Along with the big film goes a snobbery of the small film. Producers and directors will sometimes tell you, with an unnec-essary defensiveness, that they are only making the hundred-and-sixty-minute, wide screen, stereophonic, full-colour movie as a prelude to the ninety-minute, small screen, black-and-white film which is what they really enjoy. But film-makers easily become prisoners of their own elaborate creations, dragged along at the chariot-wheels of another Roman triumph; and, as some of them readily admit, a director who has moved into this area may well find it easier, in future, to raise £2,000,000 or so rather than a mere quarter of a million. In this world of status symbols, to go smaller is to appear to go down.

The blockbuster policy may well have sound commercial logic on its side, but it has meant some significant changes in the whole attitude to film-making. Up to ten years ago, when the very long and expensive film was still something entirely excep-tional, the film-maker usually reckoned to turn out a movie every year or so. Now a David Lean, for instance, shows us a film in 1957 and another in 1962; and the sheer length of time it takes to produce a *Lawrence of Arabia* means that creative energy has somehow to be conserved over two or three years. Small wonder that few people have the stamina simply to keep the whole thing going; that one feels a general slackening of the creative drive – of that urge, even, to a grandiose, outrageous, and in its way magnificent vulgarity which used to be part of the make-up of Hollywood.

Below the level of the very big pictures, the philosophy of size still operates. The old ambition was to tell a story in a sharp ninety minutes, cutting corners where necessary, making every shot do its proper job of work. Now everything moves more slowly; to such an extent, indeed, that one learns in talking to a Hollywood writer that the comedy script which in 1939 would have made up into a compact ninety-minute film would now, if reshot *exactly as it stands*, automatically run a good two hours. Dialogue is actually spoken more deliberately; time goes in showing off the scenery (why not? – it probably cost money to get there); nothing is thrown away or left unexplained; and bone and muscle too easily disintegrate under the fat of production values. *Necessary* slowness, as one encounters it in the films of an Antonioni or a Satyajit Ray, is one thing; inflationary tactics another. And part of the problem for contemporary Hollywood is that so few of its really big films look as though anyone got any fun out of making them.

The urge to make big statements on bigger screens has caught up with many of the major American talents. Vincente Minnelli, a painter *manqué*, humorist, and master of the dancing image, has moved from *Under the Clock* and *The Pirate* to *Lust for Life* and *The Four Horsemen of the Apocalypse*. His colour sense and sureness about where to place the camera survive; but hardly the old glancing lightness and discretion. Fred Zinnemann, humane and generous in his sympathies in post-war films like *The Men* (about a paraplegic ward) and *Teresa* (an Italian war bride in New York), preserves these qualities in heavy-weight literary adaptations such as *The Nun's Story* and *The Sundowners*. He no longer, though, gives you quite that rare sense of an artist with the ability to say a simple thing simply. John Huston, the taut, virile film-maker of *The Maltese Falcon* and

The Treasure of Sierra Madre, the director for stories of for-lorn hopes, criminal conspiracies, and the tensions of betrayal, allows his talent to sprawl across the windy wastes of *The Roots of Heaven* or *The Misfits*. An occasional flashing sequence (like the mustang round-up in *The Misfits*) breaks through as a re-minder that he still keeps his unerring eye for the way people look in action.

These film-makers, and others who have followed the big-picture route, like Otto Preminger, George Stevens, William Wyler, remain Hollywood's master craftsmen. They command unlimited technical resources, and the confidence to exploit them. They work with cameramen, cutters, art directors who have set the standards for the world. But they are inhabitants of a nervous industry, which has put its trust in best-sellers, hit plays, pre-sold properties, and in doing so cut down on the area in which they can be really creative. 'The biggest, most expen-sive electric-train set anyone could be given to play with,' Nicholas Ray has called the movies. But when the train is pulling a few million pounds of shareholders' money, and the fortunes of a company may be riding with it, what director could risk running it off the rails by taking chances, breaking through this standard of intimidating, unquestioned professionalism into the headier and more dangerous regions of creative risk?

In theory, the opportunities seemed to be there. Until the late forties, the 'Big Five' Hollywood film companies (Fox, Warner Brothers, M.G.M., Paramount, R.K.O.-Radio) had been 'vertical' combines. Like the Rank Organization in Britain, they acted as producers, distributors, and exhibitors, with an inevitable obligation to provide a steady flow of films for their own cinema chains. In 1950, however, after years of legal batt-ling against the Anti-Trust Laws, a Supreme Court ruling en-forced 'divorcement', splitting off the business of production and distribution from theatre ownership. The interests of the two sides of the industry, consequently, had ceased to be identical at precisely the moment when the crucial economic readjustment began; and the result was double-edged. Firstly, when it came to the point of reducing production, companies found it easier, and financially a great deal safer, to lease their studio space and facilities to independent production units and to cut down their own immediate involvement in film-making. Secondly, since they no longer had a direct relationship with the cinemas, there was more inducement for them to move into TV, or to make some quick cash by selling off their stocks of old films to television.

This opening of the door to independent production provided, in theory, opportunities for risk and adventure; and proved, when it came to the point, that producers, directors, and actors, left to themselves, would make much the same kind of films that they had been working on for their studio overlords. And independence, of course, is a word subject to infinite qualification. The producer still has to come to terms with his financial backers and with distributors; he has to deal with agents, with their philosophy of the 'package deal', whereby to acquire the particular script he wants he may have to take a director or a star along with it; he has to manipulate all the complex human factors that go into the making of a film. If he lacks the burden of studio overheads, he also cannot afford the luxury of making commercial blunders, confident that whatever happens there will still be a studio behind him. If he operates cheaply, he knows that the sensational subject will be the quickest seller; if he works on the big scale, he competes for the latest best-sellers along with the studios. He knows that bankers more readily advance finance if a big star name is attached to a picture; and the stars, freed from the long-term contracts holding them to a particular studio, demand their sizeable cut of the profits. Actors and directors roam from one assignment to the next, from one studio to another. Power shifts from the studio bosses, the paternal despots who used to control their careers, to the agents who negotiate their contracts. The most celebrated of all the agencies, M.C.A., moved into both film and television production, until forced in 1962, by a legal decision, to decide between the agency business and the production business. The era of independence has also proved, strikingly, the era of the agent.

Independence has gone with the move away from Hollywood itself. New York is once again a production centre, with producer–directors such as Elia Kazan preferring to run their companies from the East. Increasingly, Hollywood organizations transfer themselves, permanently or for a single picture, to Europe. Samuel Bronston, producer of *El Cid* and *King of Kings*, has his studio in Spain; Sam Spiegel, most peripatetic of producers, made *The Bridge on the River Kwai* and *Lawrence of Arabia* in Europe and on Eastern locations; John Huston's *Freud* and Billy Wilder's *One, Two, Three* were shot in Germany; some Hollywood film or other is more or less permanently in residence at Cinecittà, in Rome; Seven Arts, one of the major independent production organizations, moves easily between America and Britain. The list is endless: sometimes a film is made overseas because the stars prefer it that way, sometimes to get round taxation or to use blocked foreign currency, sometimes because, however much European prices may rise, a spectacular set can still be built more cheaply or an army unit hired for a battle scene. And this, emphatically, inescapably, and, in so far as one can use the word, permanently, has become the new pattern. Hollywood used to mean Hollywood; now the stars commute from Switzerland, the deals are signed in London, and the movies get made in Rome or Tokyo.

At any given moment, there are likely to be more television series than movies in active production at a big Hollywood studio. Three-quarters of Hollywood's studio population, it has been estimated, now work in television and not in films. In the old days, small companies turning out cut-price Westerns made them two at a time – same bar-room set, same actors, a frugal minimum of changes in clothes and dialogue. Now TV companies, no less brisk and more efficient, turn out the same kind of Westerns, in the same studios, as likely as not with the same technicians.

Television did more than this: it supplied the film companies with a market for their old films and enabled them to realize on assets which had previously added up, commercially if not historically, to so many cans of dead celluloid. In Britain, the film industry has come together rather effectively to keep films as far as possible off the television screens, the fear being that if the movies shown on TV are not too decrepit, they keep people at home who might otherwise be in the cinemas. In America the barriers fell with a crash in 1955, when R.K.O.-Radio ceased production and was sold to a company whose interest lay at least partly in the acquisition of TV rights in the old movies. (The studio itself was bought by Desilu, the TV production company which had made a fortune out of *I Love Lucy*.) If one company had opened the doors to television, others might as well do the same; and by 1957 it could be estimated that more than 10,000 cinema films had become available to TV. An expanding industry, desperate for any material it could lay its hands on, had come to terms with a contracting one, equally hard up for cash to see it through the worst years.

The sale of assets to television; the sale of part of the studio lands for housing developments; the move overseas, the so-called 'runaway' productions fiercely resented by the cinema labour unions: these have been symptoms of Hollywood's decline. Big companies have appointed production executives, thrown them out when they failed to come up with some incontrovertible formula for success, and tried again with someone else. Things can never again be as they were, because it is beyond the power of anyone in the studios to call back the lost audience to the cinemas. Hollywood has lost so much since the end of the war that it is important also to bear in mind what it has held on to: the ability to make pictures for the world.

5. Production Values

When Jean-Luc Godard made *À Bout de Souffle*, throwing his film like a hand-grenade into the audience, he dedicated it, not entirely as a joke, to Monogram Pictures. The name carried an evocative load of associations for every enthusiast of the Hollywood B-picture, a reminder not only of the indestructible Bowery Boys, but of all the little thrillers which used to turn up in the lower half of the bill. And the young French directors, devoted to an idea of America derived from Faulkner and Dashiell Hammett, paid their tribute also to the American B-picture, the movies which never got bogged down in dialogue or slowed up by any expression of ideas, but at their best constructed a kind of underworld culture of their own out of the very shabbiness and familiarity of their material.

The American critic Manny Farber gave the title 'Underground Films' to an influential article, published in 1957, in which he lamented the passing of 'the long-neglected action directors' (he named Raoul Walsh, Howard Hawks, William Wellman, William Keighley, Anthony Mann) in favour of what he rudely called 'the water buffaloes of film art' (George Stevens, Billy Wilder, Vittorio de Sica). The critic, he said, would choose for praise 'a picture backed by studio build-up, agreement among his colleagues, a lay-out in *Life* magazine . . . and a list of ingredients that anyone's unsophisticated aunt in Oakland can spot as a distinguished film'. Meanwhile, the underground directors would be chiselling away at projects which

are neither experimental, liberal, slick, spectacular, low-budget, epical, improving, or flagrantly commercial. . . . The action directors accept the role of hack so that they can involve themselves with expedience and tough-guy insight in all types of action. The important thing is not so much the banal-seeming journeys to nowhere that make up the stories, but the tunnelling that goes on inside the classic Western-gangster incidents and stock hoodlum–dogface–cowboy types.

Critics have not done the action directors justice, even if those who have celebrated their films have sometimes overdone it ('The Hawks film is as good on the mellifluous grace of the impudent American hard rock as can be found in any art work' – Farber), or found themselves sentimentalizing over their essentially unsentimental subject. The 'underground movie' kept its back turned to art and got on with telling a story of murder or gang treachery or the range wars of the West, using the screen flexibly and confidently to make small, shrewd points about people and places. Now that it is indeed passing, with the growing self-consciousness which attacks film-makers and their employers, the feeling that simply to do this is somehow not enough, it looks like the most genuinely and valuably indigenous form of Hollywood cinema.

Essentially, the people who made these films moved about easily in the world of their shabby subjects. Cheap boxing-matches, run-down hotel rooms, private detectives' offices, police stations, bar-rooms, cars driving in the daytime down the four-lane highways or nosing through city streets on rainy nights, hold-ups among the dustbins of alleyways: these were the settings and the ingredients. The heroine was usually discovered propped against a piano, singing some insolent dirge.

The hero was a cynic who had been pushed around once too often. In the late forties, all kinds of directors worked this territory; and a film like Howard Hawks's *The Big Sleep*, with its casual, painful violence, its hard, sparring dialogue and blank-faced humour, now serves as well as any to epitomize an era. As Raymond Chandler said of his own work in pulp fiction, the principle was that when you were in doubt about what to do next, you opened a door on a man with a gun in his hand. *The Big Sleep* has one death which even the people making the film were not sure about: was it, they asked Chandler as the writer of the novel, a case of murder or suicide? But the violence, if casual, was not sensational. One remembers the films rather for their settings – the detective's office, with the neon light flicking off and on across the street, the sweltering conservatory in which only the desiccated old millionaire can breathe in comfort, the gun battles in the car headlights, and the sad little man (Elisha Cook Jun., that prototype of sad little men) dying among the office filing-cabinets.

These films, of course, had their literary origins and equivalents in the novels of writers like Chandler and Dashiell Hammett, and, perhaps at one remove, Hemingway. They were romantically tough but not soft-centred, like some of the movies that followed, in which criminals pined for the quiet country life and psychiatry rode the range. When the Western belatedly discovered Freud and the thriller became blankly sadistic, the action directors were collaborating in the destruction of their own kind of cinema. Instead of moving casually around in surroundings they had made their own, they began to observe from the outside, to comment and underline. The 'underground' film needs to remain underground in the interests of its own survival.

Self-importance has been the bogey of Hollywood film-making in the last ten years or so. Part of this, ironically, may be discerned as a side-effect of Hollywood's post-war liberalism –

the urge, fostered by a producer such as Dore Schary, to use cinema for social education. But brave intentions, in the climate of an industry, produced cautious, right-thinking films: it shows no great daring to attack capital punishment, for instance, if the scales are to be weighted by special pleading on behalf of an innocent victim. At the same time, studios wanted, and from a business point of view probably needed, to make their movies look important. An adaptation of a best-seller, carefully cast to spread its appeal across the widest possible range, with a couple of stars for the teenagers and a couple more for their parents, could be more or less pre-sold. 'Book-of-the-month' cinema moved in.

It is not very surprising that among the directors who have shown the most staying-power have been the professional cynics, men like Alfred Hitchcock and Billy Wilder who operate on their own arrogant terms, and whose box-office formulas are so good that no one tries to tamper with them. Hitchcock's career offers total refutation of the theory that film-makers, like boxers, never come back. He has moved through periods of slow-motion film-making (as in the late forties, with pictures like *Rope* and *The Paradine Case*) and then returned from these tedious safaris to show in a *Strangers on a Train*, a *Trouble with Harry*, a *North by Northwest*, that his hand remains as steady, his humour as insolent, his mastery of the camera as complete as ever. Hitchcock has always been a past-master of the planned incongruity: a crop-dusting aeroplane comes out of a quiet sky to spray bullets at a man standing alone in the stubble; a corpse, impudent and accusing, lies amid the red autumn leaves of a New England wood; a near-strangling ruffles the polite surface of a diplomatic party. Murder in the United Nations building; at a funfair (with, as an extra refinement, the whole scene reflected in a lens of the victim's spectacles); in a run-down motel; in a New York block of flats, with James Stewart across the courtyard to witness it. Hitchcock looks on, with a compulsive curiosity about the way people behave and a school-boy's delight in catching them out. A cigarette ground out in a fried egg (in *To Catch a Thief*) becomes as much of a shock image as a shrivelled old mummy concealed in a cellar (in *Psycho*). Hitchcock gloats over his own effects, draws them out like a man pulling at a piece of elastic, then snaps it abruptly shut in the audience's face. A surprising number of case-hardened critics were shocked by *Psycho*, that sick joke in a Gothic-horror for-mat, as though they felt that this time he had gone too far. But for Hitchcock, part of the fascination lies in seeing what he can get away with – technically, as in *Rear Window*, in which all the action was seen from a single vantage point, or thematically, as in *Psycho*. He is the complete movie-maker.

Billy Wilder takes a similar pleasure in choosing a patch of thin ice, from the point of view of public response, and cutting some expert circles in it. He made a serious film about alcoholism (*The Lost Weekend*) at a time when, incredible as it now seems, this still appeared a fairly daring thing to do. His comic subjects – the sustained transvestist joke of *Some Like It Hot*, the post-war Berlin of fraternization and the black market (*A Foreign Affair*), the Berlin crisis of 1961 (*One, Two, Three*), the amalgam of sex and office politics in *The Apartment* – have generally been exer-cises, more or less successful, more or less desperate, in seeing what might be done with a bad-taste joke, or how to be vulgar *and* funny. None of these films, though, could match the style of *Sunset Boulevard*, that baroque confrontation of the new Hollywood, in the person of a not very successful and moderately corruptible young writer, with the old, as symbolized by Gloria Swanson, the lost star from the lost twenties with her empty swimming pool, her director turned butler (Erich von Stro-heim), her delusions, and her splendid memories. *Sunset Boulevard* has all Wilder's cold intelligence, knowingness, relish for details carefully observed and memorized, and adds a grandeur of its own. 'I'm big,' cries the desolate star. 'It's the pictures that have got small. . . . We didn't need dialogue, we had faces then.' Well, and sadly, yes.

Alfred Hitchcock, Billy Wilder, and other veterans such as John Ford, with his magnificent string of Westerns in the first post-war years (*My Darling Clementine*, *She Wore a Yellow Ribbon*, *Wagonmaster*) and his abiding feeling for an old, emotive Americanism, are directors who have grown up with the myths. They can kick the movies around. They are not scared of repetition, or self-parody, or the obvious. Ford sets a line of cavalrymen riding along the horizon, with one of the old Western songs roaring up on the sound track, and the image sustains all its quality of romantic release. Confidently, easily, unerringly, it is put before us; and there is a relaxed assurance about the film-making of Hollywood's old guard that one doesn't quite find anywhere else in the world. Directors like this, you feel, put the machinery together: they don't have to keep taking it to pieces to check on whether it still works.

These film-makers, and others among the older generation (George Cukor, for instance, peerless director of actresses, and decorative stylist, or Frank Capra, once the cinema's spokesman for the New Deal) have supremely the movie-making faculty. They put pictures on the screen, without concerning themselves over-much about where they are going or what may happen to them when they get there. It is a confidence which has not been passed down. Among the directors who came later to film-making, there may be more drive, more urgency, more sense of importance and occasion, but less stamina. George Stevens, one senses, would never embark on a film without the conscious intention of producing a master-work. And although he has twice come at least within striking distance (*A Place in the Sun* and *Shane*), the deliberation and unremitting effort, the doggedness of his style, with its suggestion that every scene has been covered from every conceivable and inconceivable angle, can produce on less happy occasions the effect of a car with the brakes on straining at a slope. *The Diary of Anne Frank* shows how easily the small, intimate subject can get lost inside the big movie. Elia Kazan, domesticator of the Method in Hollywood, does not strain: he bores into Tennessee Williams (*A Streetcar Named Desire*, *Baby Doll*), or commercial television (*A Face in the Crowd*), or stevedores' battles (*On the Waterfront*), or adolescent agonies (*East of Eden*, *Splendour in the Grass*). He usually emerges with some clearly lighted Freudian truth; and on the way he finds an immense amount that is vigorous and stimulating for his actors to do. Marlon Brando has never looked a more exciting actor than in his films for Kazan. Yet, at the end, one seldom feels that one has been watching very much more than a dazzling display of muscle-flexing, with some inspired performances on the side. The work top-heavy with significance, or the work with too little going on beneath a brilliant surface: these sum up a good deal of the history of the art-plus-entertainment industry, and not only in Hollywood.

Younger directors, either those who came up in the first post-war wave or those who followed them in the fifties – Nicholas Ray, Robert Aldrich, Robert Wise, Stanley Kubrick, Richard Quine – have mostly pursued, with however many personal divergences, the seemingly inescapable trend of the times. From small pictures, made with devotion and individuality (Ray's *They Live By Night*, Wise's *The Set-Up*, Kubrick's *The Killing*), they advance by gradual and not always easy stages towards the spectaculars (*King of Kings*, *West Side Story*, *Spartacus*) in which creative personality has to fight to make itself felt. And it is because of this artist's fight to impose his own ideas and drives on material made cumbersome by the fat of production values that these later films so often lack the muscularity or the grace of the earlier ones, made when the film-maker really was right on top of his material. Stanley Kubrick's *Lolita*, which charted the course of Humbert Humbert's obsession with such wit and desperation, such controlled intensity and stabbing irony, revived a lot of confidence. Here, again, was a film which contributed creative pleasure, the sense of the director's own excitement in making his tools work for him. John Franken-heimer's *The Manchurian Candidate* did the same, assuming the existence of an audience alert to quirkishness, fancy, those rough edges of personality which the too-careful production likes to iron out. Both films, it might be noted, managed to find that audience.

Because films must now be made with the entire world market in mind (and 200 million people a week, all over the world, are estimated to watch American movies), Hollywood is inclined to stress its own ambassadorial role. When, as in the case of *The Blackboard Jungle*, an American representative overseas complains of the view foreign audiences are getting of the United States through its films, the studios at once react defensively. But for whatever reason, as a long-range conse-quence of the McCarthyist years, or as more immediate evidence of the pressures under which Hollywood talents have to work, or as a larger symptom of the dissatisfactions America's creative minds feel about the way we live now, Hollywood has certainly been giving its world public some massively disenchanted comments on the American scene.

In film after film, the same targets have been assailed: the poor American mother, long since given a flying kick from her pedestal; the breakdown of communication between the gener-ations; the miseries of growing up in the United States; the corruptions infecting society. Sinclair Lewis revealed that Main Street was full of Babbitts; Hollywood in the last few years has focused on the neurotic private face of Babbittry. We have been told that children cannot talk to their parents (*Rebel Without a Cause*); that possessive mothers drive their daughters to the madhouse (*Splendour in the Grass*); that big business is not all it might be (*Executive Suite*); that commercial television is worse (*A Face in the Crowd*); that small towns are the worst of the lot (*Peyton Place*); that the deep South is the breeding-ground of insanity (practically any adaptation from Tennessee Williams); that blackmail extends to the floor of the Senate (*Advise and Consent*); that even presidents are not above suspicion (*Advise and Consent* again). The tone has varied from the cool (Otto Preminger) to the nervously intense (Nicholas Ray); but the common currency of America's 'serious' movie-making has been disillusionment. The cinema of social awareness, which Hollywood's has always been, has turned inwards; the dream factory has gone over to the mass-produced nightmare.

This area of Hollywood film-making has seemed obsessed with Freud – or with the idea that it *ought* to be obsessed with Freud, which amounts in practice to the same thing. The cynical interpretation sometimes put forward is that a link may thus be forged between Hollywood's deep-rooted Puritanism, its share of the Pilgrim Fathers' inheritance, and an equally deep-rooted acquisitive instinct. If films like *Butterfield 8* or *The Chapman Report* are case-histories, and therefore therapeutic, then they cannot be fairly accused of sensation-mongering. But this would be to attribute too much conscious and cynical motive to the film-makers. If all the studies of frustration and desperation, with Big Daddy and (even worse) Big Mother hovering vulture-like over their broods, provide a sociological field-day, it is not because they are cynical but because they are sincere. When a writer like William Inge tacks backwards and forwards, in *The Dark at the Top of the Stairs* and *Splendour in the Grass* and *All Fall Down*, over the hazards of family life, one does not doubt that he believes America is full of unhappy families.

It looked, for a short while in the middle fifties, as though television – of all unlikely sources – might bring something more outward-going and optimistic, as well as a new approach to the perennial problem of how to let the quiet individual voice make itself heard in the uproar. *Marty*, the story of a Bronx

73

butcher's love-affair with a plain girl, and more specifically of his discovery of the areas in which happiness was possible for him, established a trend. Rumour insisted, rightly or not, that this adaptation of Paddy Chayefsky's television play was intended by the Hecht–Lancaster company as a low-budget experiment to be set for tax purposes against more costly productions. When the critics took the picture up, and Ernest Borgnine won an Oscar nomination, enough was spent on promotion and advertising to lift the film into a more expensive bracket.

Paddy Chayefsky, with his reporter's ear for dialogue and his flair for an essentially Jewish kind of genre writing, remained a playwright for the small screen. When he tried to extend his range, in the script for *The Goddess*, it became evident that he needed the kind of concentration TV had enforced. *Marty* and *Bachelor Party*, both directed by Delbert Mann, looked sharply at small sectors of New York life: the young men who realize that they are never going to amount to very much, the melancholy pleasures of a night on the town. But the personality behind the films was very much the writer's; and the group of films which came to the cinema via television, lively though some of them were, could not shake off this dependence on dialogue. They brought into the cinema a whole group of young directors who have since proved their adaptability in Hollywood – Sidney Lumet, who did the jury-room drama *Twelve Angry Men*, John Frankenheimer, whose *The Young Stranger* turned an unusually sympathetic eye on angry adolescence, Martin Ritt, whose *A Man is Ten Feet Tall* treated a relationship between a callow young white man and a balanced, responsible Negro. Television, which demands high-speed work, resourcefulness, and an ability to improvise, has become one of the cinema's training-grounds; and the television play, which was then at its height and attracting writers who found here the challenge of a new form, a kind of short-story drama of urban life, brought a new source of material into the American cinema at a time when it was badly needed. But the films, although made relatively cheaply, proved not quite cheap enough. Specialized audiences might enjoy the jury-room interchange of *Twelve Angry Men*, but it was too unassuming for a mass market and a little too expensive to pay its way among the kind of public it could attract.

In any case, the appetite was for stronger stuff. Partly owing to a relaxation of the pressures of the Production Code (the industry's censorship system, still sometimes mistakenly called, after its first administrator, the Hays Code) Hollywood gained considerably in freedom during the middle fifties. The Code, which must be read to be believed, laid down all kinds of elaborate prohibitions, many of which film-makers had been ingeniously circumventing over the years. Pressures to relax the Code sprang partly from the desire to give the cinema another weapon in its armoury against television, partly from the effect of a deliberate flanking attack on censorship bans mounted by independent producers such as Otto Preminger. When Preminger's comedy *The Moon is Blue* was released without a Code seal of approval, and notoriety was found to pay off, a lesson had been spelled out.

The sanctity of marriage and the home shall be upheld [the Code heroically asserted]. Pictures shall not infer [sic] that low forms of sex relationship are the accepted or common thing. . . . Adultery and illicit sex, sometimes necessary plot material, must not be explicitly treated, or justified, or presented attractively. . . .

How remote and innocent it seems.

Film-makers and critics had for years been attacking this restrictive censorship because of the evasions and dishonesties it fostered.

The prime effect of the Code [wrote Gilbert Seldes] is to create a sexual morality which no moralist, no great religious leader, no church has ever tolerated. It is as mythical as the social and economic contrivances of the movies are. . . .

Theoretically, Hollywood's release from this enforced chastity would point the way to a more grown-up and consequently more responsible cinema, so putting the American industry on a level footing with Europe. In fact, the Code was relaxed at the moment when economic pressures were all towards sensationalism. Drug addiction (previously one of the forbidden subjects) yielded a new kind of problem picture; a series of 'True Confessions' movies charted the tearful remorse of reformed alcoholics; Gina Lollobrigida and Elizabeth Taylor played call-girls; cannibalism had a mild fling in *Suddenly Last Summer*; William Wyler remade *The Children's Hour* (as *The Loudest Whisper*) with the Lesbian references out in the open; and so on, and so on.

No one was noticeably shocked by these films; and some handicaps of film-making in a permissive climate of public opinion soon enough become apparent. The artist demands freedom, but a right of challenge and dissent may work out better than a free-for-all.

It's in the interests of the producers [Jean Renoir shrewdly commented] to maintain a certain standard of morality, since if they don't do this immoral films won't sell. . . . I am sure that the great quality of the early American films sprang from an American puritanism which put up barriers to American passions. When we saw Lillian Gish, who was probably going to be assaulted by the villain, we trembled. . . . Today, what can you do with the rape of a girl who has already made love to the entire town?

The artist might wonder what to do; the commercial entrepreneur need not bother: and it is the catchpenny level of exploitation which ultimately depresses conditions all round. As the magazine fiction of the screen moved from its *Saturday Evening Post* into its *Confidential* era, so the stars who had sustained the old brand – Joan Crawford, mink-coated and pistol-packing, the astringent Barbara Stanwyck, Bette Davis, heroine of the sublime slogan 'nobody's as good as Bette when she's bad' – quietly began to bow out.

Producers nowadays repeatedly grumble that there are only about half a dozen surviving stars who really count at the box-office; and that these are pricing themselves out of the market. In fact, the idea of the indispensable star was probably always a bit of a myth, encouraged by the big studios at a time when they held the indispensables safely under contract. The essence of the pre-war stars, however, was their durability. Clark Gable and Humphrey Bogart, James Stewart, Joan Crawford, Mary Astor, Katharine Hepburn all had (and have) the allure of the indestructible personality. Misused by their employers, flung into disastrous parts which sent their box-office stock crashing, they would always come back, firmly instructing the cameramen on how best to light their close-ups, commanding their films and on occasion their directors.

The stars of the fifties and sixties are more vulnerable, partly because Hollywood's pursuit of a substantially teenage public encourages the old identification principle to operate on a narrower front. Actors are old at twenty-five and positively doddering at thirty: one film (Leo McCarey's *Rally Round the Flag, Boys*) whose stars were the still agile Paul Newman and Joanne Woodward, actually threw in another, younger pair for obvious purposes of teenage identification. When the whole thing gets out of hand, however, as it did with James Dean, Hollywood draws back in alarm. The piles of mail collected in the offices of Warner Brothers for a dead actor; the models of his death mask and the scraps torn from his car; the people who chose to regard themselves as inheritors of his spirit and the people who refused to believe that he was dead at all: these made up the Dean cult, and it was essentially and lugubriously a posthumous one.

Dean starred in only three films, in one of which (George Stevens's *Giant*) he was unsympathetically cast. But *East of*

Eden, and to a still greater extent Nicholas Ray's *Rebel Without a Cause*, with its feeling for adolescence as a conspiracy, its air of special pleading for a generation, set up an electric current between actor and audience. Dean suggested infinite vulnerability; he wore his leather jacket not with defiance but in fearful protest. Where Marlon Brando communicated (notably in *On the Waterfront*) the surly strength of a fighter, Dean kept the world warily at a distance, used, repeatedly, a nervous gesture like that of a shying horse, sat huddled as if against the cold. The other great myth star, Marilyn Monroe, played lost child or resilient waif, and seemed to bring with her on to the screen, whatever part she played, the bundle of tensions and confusions, aspirations and regrets, which made up her private life. The star as victim, as someone with a softer shell than the rest of us; the star as misfit – society finds, unfailingly, the particular symbols it needs.

Hollywood was blamed, inevitably, for Marilyn Monroe's death: a shocked public opinion, reminded that real people lurk behind the myths so assiduously publicized, needed a villain. And Hollywood did in fact seem roused to a sense of guilt; the more easily, perhaps, because of the odd sort of inferiority complex under which the industry seems to labour, the feelings of inadequacy its artists openly voice when they look at films from Europe, the doubts about just where their cinema is heading. What needs to be recaptured, more than anything, is the commercial confidence to be optimistic; to move easily again in a whole area of film-making which at its lower levels provides unpretentious entertainment and at its higher levels gives us the kind of thing that Hollywood does superlatively and that Europe does hardly at all.

This industry, in fact, has always existed to confound those pedants who would like to think that the serious business of art and the frivolities of entertainment can be neatly pigeon-holed in their separate compartments. People who regard musicals or

Westerns or thrillers as by definition limited genres have never really managed to come to terms with Hollywood. They would prefer its film-makers to devote themselves to subjects with tangible evidence of serious purpose. They want a solid cinema with its feet on the ground, and they do not know quite what to do with a *Singin' in the Rain*, a *Wagonmaster*, a *Mildred Pierce*, which are so patently of the cinema, are in fact the stuff of the cinema. Hollywood has ceded a bit of ground to them in recent years, with its taste for the pre-packaged best-seller. It has surrendered the confidence to do unimportant things with style, the drive which makes possible both an Andy Hardy *and* a *Citizen Kane*.

Economically, the American industry is precluded from taking the way of the European film-makers. A factory cannot be turned overnight into a cottage industry, and Hollywood could no more operate on a policy of a few high-calibre pictures than Detroit could turn itself over to Rolls-Royces. Somehow, though, this industry has let itself slide into an uneasy middle age. Half a dozen men of great talent, inevitably past the creative peak of their careers, continue to turn out pictures with the easy assurance of an earlier age. The best of their juniors are liable to be wandering about Europe, caught up in that cinema inter-nationalism in which director and cameraman and stars may only be able to communicate through an interpreter. Committed to an existence of big hotels, rented villas, international airports, these directors have to struggle to retain contact with their material – something more essential, and more difficult, for the film-maker than any other artist. Even in America, they come to a subject in the manner of a tourist. And meanwhile the studios, with an air of exhausted optimism, remake their own successes – a new *Four Horsemen of the Apocalypse*, a new *Mutiny on the Bounty*, a new *State Fair* – in a form of doleful tribute to the old gods of the box-office.

But the portents are not all discouraging: the American

79

industry has any amount of talent, fighting for opportunities or waiting to be put to use. New directors arrive from television or elsewhere. And there is the object-lesson of United Artists, the company which has grown rich by acting as distributor for most of the major independent production outfits and which recognizes the advantages of diversity. Hollywood as the original film capital is more or less played out; Hollywood as a symbol survives. Out of the whole long and immensely difficult process of adjustment ought to come a new American cinema, provided that the talents capable of creating it are not bedevilled by all the problems which have more to do with symbolic status than with the actual business of making pictures.

6. Taken from the French

If commercial film-making traditionally means Hollywood, quality film-making traditionally means France; if Hollywood's directors look longingly towards the greater freedoms of Europe, it is to France that they look first. Every tyro cinéaste, becoming aware of horizons beyond the English-speaking cinema, has probably gone through his Francophil stage; and rightly so. Infuriating though it may often seem to the rest of us, they do order some things better; not least because, at an early stage in film history, the French intellectuals decided to take up the cinema. In too many countries the cinema, like television, has had to work its slow passage towards respectability by way of the nursery and the servants' quarters, picking up the occasional kind word when it has gone in for literary adaptation, ignored when it has been most thoroughly itself. In France, for a long time now, the film-maker has been under no obligation to prove that he, too, may be an artist.

This confidence is reflected, inevitably, in the kind of people attracted to the medium. There does not seem much doubt that film-makers like René Clair and Jean Renoir could have made as great an impact had they chosen some other field to work in;

and as writers and commentators they have extended the literature of the screen. Hollywood film-makers are always complaining that they are isolated, tucked away in their Californian retreat while the political life of the nation centres on Washington and the cultural life on New York. Even in England, with the major studios all concentrated within an hour's driving time of London, film-makers have a way of meeting mainly other film-makers. In France, for forty years or so, the interchange of ideas has operated freely. It would be considered very odd indeed here if Iris Murdoch or Harold Pinter were suddenly to turn up as a film director; but it does not seem particularly improbable in France that Alain Robbe-Grillet should decide he would like to make a film.

The point should not be pushed too hard: a high degree of literacy is not something every film-maker needs to have, any more than every painter. To the individual it may even be a handicap. But to an industry as a whole it brings an enviable solidarity. The film-maker need never feel that he lives on a kind of cultural backstairs, cut off from all the grander artistic doings at the front of the house. Critical writing assumes a more alert readership; audiences are likely to be more responsive. Whatever problems the film-maker encounters, and economically the French cinema has gone through some chaotic years, they will not as a rule be those of combating inertia.

At the end of the war, however, France's cinema still remained frozen in the painful attitudes imposed by the Occupation. Directors had retreated to the comparative safety of the past (Marcel Carné with *Les Visiteurs du Soir* and *Les Enfants du Paradis*, Claude Autant-Lara with *Douce*); Henri-George Clouzot's *Le Corbeau*, a study of the suspicions and hatreds unleashed in a provincial town by a series of anonymous letters, had offered the Nazis unintended ammunition on the corruption of France; René Clair, Jean Renoir, and Julien Duvivier had spent the war years in the United States; and the film which displayed the most formidable of the French cinema's new talents, Robert Bresson's *Les Dames du Bois de Boulogne*, remained largely unseen and largely unadmired.

When Jean Cocteau's *L'Éternel Retour*, made in 1943, eventually reached London three years later, critics grumbled that the blonde lovers (Jean Marais and Madeleine Sologne) in this version of the Tristan and Isolde legend had a disconcertingly Teutonic look.

The pervading mood of defeatism sublimating itself in death . . . must have made it a pleasure for the Nazis to give permission for the production [wrote Richard Winnington with sulky injustice]. There it all is, the whole dolorous bag of tricks . . . often superbly beautiful in its execution, but rotted. . . .

But if English Puritanism was not quite sure what to make of Cocteau, the danger signals came through much more clearly in the work of Marcel Carné. His *Le Jour se lève* and *Quai des Brumes* had been masterworks of pre-war romantic fatalism, with Jean Gabin watching the time ticking away in his besieged room and Michèle Morgan, wan and rain-coated, haunting that waterfront café. But when Carné and his collaborator Jacques Prévert heated up yet another brew of luxuriant melancholia in the post-war *Les Portes de la Nuit*, with one of Prévert's death-symbol characters stalking the streets of Paris, fatalism began to look like affectation. We had been there once too often.

Clair, Carné, and Renoir had been the three great names of French pre-war cinema – always excepting the dead Jean Vigo. Two of these reputations have lost ground during the last ten years; one has soared. In 1952, when *Sight and Sound* invited critics to name the ten best films in cinema history, Carné's *Le Jour se lève* took seventh place and Clair's *Le Million* tenth. Ten years later, in a similar poll, the two films mustered only four votes between them, which is probably a fair indication of how the popularity index has shifted. Carné and Prévert had made one of the cinema's great creative partnerships; and Carné in recent years, trying rather forlornly in a film like *Les Tricheurs* to show that he too has something to say about the younger generation, has had the melancholy air of an artist marooned in time, while the currents of France's new cinema swirl around him.

René Clair's films must have afforded more sheer pleasure than those of almost any other director one cares to name, which makes it seem the more unjust that this immensely talented artist should currently be going through a critical eclipse, partly because his qualities – all the perfectionist virtues of precision, elegance, conscious grace and good manners – are antipathetic to the younger generation of French directors. But Clair has been a perfectionist in small things: his enchanting Paris of *Sous les Toits* and *Le Quatorze Juillet* also remains sealed off in time, a magical and unchanging city which no one can now return to. His films since the return to France include one of his best in *Les Grandes Manœuvres*: a beautifully Stendhalian opening of a regimental parade through a provincial garrison town moves into the story of a seduction undertaken for a bet, which slowly modulates into a tragedy of lost love. Even here, however, Clair preserved his intellectual detachment, that aloofness which is part of his cool and fastidious talent. Apart from *Le Silence est d'or*, with its entranced evocation of a silent-film studio at work, his major post-war films – *La Beauté du Diable*, his version of the Faust legend, or *Les Belles de Nuit*, a fantasy devoted to the puncturing of nostalgic illusion – have carried powerful suggestions of disenchantment. He feels, in his own phrase, 'the disadvantages of the human condition'. Where Chaplin, even more conscious of these disadvantages, turned to the sterile bitterness of *A King in New York*, Clair retires to the heights of the French Academy and the dry satisfactions of the epigram.

In this he is at the opposite extreme from Jean Renoir, who

now towers over the French cinema like a not entirely reluctant patriarch, adored by the young directors, continually experimenting, still transparently in love with life, experience, and the cinema. Renoir made a belated return to his own country after directing *The River* in India, and *The Golden Coach* in Italy: two films which were both in colour; both erratic and sometimes careless in dialogue, performance, and construction; and both works which one could watch again and again for their sense of a setting and the effortless generosity of their response to a character. His later films have been as richly up and down: *French Can-Can*, the story of the triumph of the Moulin Rouge, taking up like *The Golden Coach* the theme of the theatre company, the music-hall, the delights of creation; *Le Déjeuner sur l'Herbe*, a frolic in which the life-force routs the theorists of a brave new world; *Le Testament du Docteur Cordelier*, an impish reworking of the Jekyll and Hyde story; *Le Caporal épinglé*, about an infinitely resilient soldier's escape from a prison camp and also about that quality of comradeship which for Renoir means life.

The great films from the thirties – *Toni, La Grande Illusion, La Règle du Jeu* – long ago established Renoir as one of the grand-masters; and a master who has never tired of innovation, so that his recent films have been made almost television-style, with two or three cameras shooting simultaneously to obtain greater flexibility. But it is only recently, now that the cinema has, as it were, grown up to him, that his films have been appreciated to the full. Thirty years ago Renoir was putting his camera outside a doorway, leaving it stationary while people moved in and out of the room, in and out of the frame; shooting in towards a world existing beyond the camera rather than filming a scene put on for its benefit. He was shooting out in the country, so that in his *Madame Bovary*, during a drive down a country lane, you can almost feel a shiver of cold as the sky darkens for rain. In the age of the consciously well-made film, with events clicking smoothly along from one carefully diagrammed 'big scene' to the next, this markedly unconcentrated style, in which objects take on value simply because they are *there*, part of the furniture of life, and not because they can be made to serve any immediate dramatic ends, seemed out of step with the times. Renoir, it was felt, made too light of his own imperfections. Lately, the cinema has gone Renoir's way: towards improvisation, observation of people being rather than doing, a sensuous response to what it feels like to be alive in a particular place at a particular moment in time. It is the perfectionists, who know all the answers before we have asked the questions, who now seem out of line.

Renoir could never be called a perfectionist, and his theories are about life rather than movies. He profoundly distrusts abstractions, and his comments on the cinema ('Great art is made by artisans and not by artists'; 'Imagination is the thing to be afraid of'; 'I don't believe in the myth of the individual') are those of a proud craftsman. Again and again, he has reminded us that he is not Auguste Renoir's son for nothing. His work, pre-eminently, has texture – a rich awareness of landscape and weather and the human form, of food and animals and sunshine. But if Renoir films like a painter, this is also because he inhabits, and on the evidence of his own biography of his father grew up in, a world in which creative energy is equated with existence itself. The immediate creative problem is always referred back to an experience of life: the painting could not be less abstract.

One of the disconcerting things about the cinema is the speed at which it burns up originality, turning bright young directors with ideas to spare into adroit technicians with an infinite capacity for disguising the fact that they no longer have anything to say that excites them creatively. Curiously (or perhaps, when one thinks of it, not so curiously), the directors who have concentrated in their films on expressing ideas rather than absorbing experience generally seem the first to feel the strain. The Renoirs survive; and also, in a national cinema always veering towards intellectualism or the merely chic, provide the counter-balance.

In France, as in any other highly organized industry, the question for the individual film-maker is how far he can afford to let himself be absorbed into a system which exists, as systems always must, to convert him into a saleable commodity. France probably has a rather higher share of enlightened investors than Britain or America, men prepared to take risks on a creative rather than a commercial reputation; its distribution system is less rigorously codified than our own, so that the difficult commercial proposition stands at least a chance of reaching a wider audience; and it has (or has had, since under the Treaty of Rome it is planned that by 1968 state aid to the film industry will taper to nothing) a system of government support with a few built-in incentives for quality film-making.

Economically, the fundamental problem confronting the French industry is thoroughly familiar to the British: how to keep the production sector of the business solvent. The French have never been anything like such persistent filmgoers as the British (according to the 1952 P.E.P. Report on the British Film Industry we were then averaging twenty-seven visits a year to the cinema per head of the population, against a modest eight in France), and television has made its inroads. To assist production, consequently, the French government operates an aid system not dissimilar in general terms to the British, while the industry works resolutely, through the Unifrance agency, to step up its exports.

All this holds a significance not merely economic. France has gone through production crises, though the number of features made annually remained tolerably stable (110 in 1951; 104 in 1961) until the 1962 crisis brought it down to 80. But sectors of her production have been geared to an export as well as a home market, with some awareness that the strongest card to be played abroad (apart from all those sad little films that

87

turn up in the British 'X' market under titles like *Mam'selle Striptease* or *The Pavements of Paris*) is a quality reputation. The lower depths of the French industry are as low as anyone's; the heights are that much higher. And a government concerned about what the cinema can do for national prestige fits into its aid system a method by which free loans or advances are made to carefully selected productions. The sums involved were never enormous and have been reduced during recent years. But if anyone wonders just how some of the more adventurous films got before the cameras at all, here is part of the answer. Advances of, say, 50,000,000 old francs to Bresson's *Un Condamné à mort s'est échappé*, or of 450,000 new francs to Resnais's *L'Année dernière à Marienbad*, bridge the gap between unimaginable risk and workable risk.

Still more important, in the whole scheme of the French cinema, has been the emphasis on co-production, mainly between France and Italy but on more exotic occasions involving tie-ups between three or four nations. A British or American film will usually be promoted by one company, or perhaps a couple: a Franco-Italian film may be backed by as many as half a dozen firms, with a key impresario who has set up the deal. All this was becoming standard form even before the Common Market; and as the film industries of Western Europe gradually come closer together there are obvious economic benefits all round. The Western European market, viewed as a single entity, is a great deal more enticing than the French, Italian, or West German markets, seen as separate units divided from each other by language barriers. Co-production formulas are now thoroughly worked out: a major star from each country; two language versions; and a film which qualifies for whatever aids and benefits each government extends to its home product.

Hence, naturally, the growing demand for bi- and tri-lingual actors. For the Italians there has been no problem, since it has been customary for them to rely heavily on dubbing in their own films. Italian actresses knew they had really arrived from the moment when they were allowed to speak from the screen with their own voices, Neapolitan accents and all; and it is now film legend that Monica Vitti's introduction to the cinema consisted in dubbing for one of the actresses in *Il Grido*. But if the Italians take the process in their stride, some French directors have been less happy both about dubbing, which robs the actor of part of his personality when it takes away his own voice, and about the way co-production can result in neutral, anonymous films without national character or idiom. In practice, however, the fact that Annie Girardot and Alain Delon play in *Rocco and his Brothers*, or Jeanne Moreau in *La Notte*, or Alida Valli in *Une Aussi Longue Absence*, can hardly be said to have done the films any harm. Purist arguments break down when confronted with actual films. In any case, international casting, international financing, fit the whole European pattern. Europe is moving towards a Common Market cinema, as industrialists like the Italian producer Dino de Laurentiis are very well aware.

But the French cinema, for all of this, has found no sure or easy way to solvency. Some of the pressures can be felt in the work of directors who have got a firm grip on the commercial ropes, as well as in the experiences of those who can offer their backers only their talent. Who were the directors one might have picked out in the French cinema of ten or twelve years ago? Claude Autant-Lara, who had consolidated his already high reputation with *Le Diable au Corps*, that harshly poetic adaptation of Radiguet's novel about a First World War love-affair. René Clément, who had followed the 1945 Resistance documentary *La Bataille du Rail* with *Jeux Interdits* and the cool comedy of *Knave of Hearts*, made in England and still probably the best feature film to be recommended to anyone who wants to see London on the screen. Yves Allegret, who was director of the glumly distinguished *Une Si Jolie Petite Plage*. Henri-Georges

89

Clouzot, who was already in the process of moving, after the excellent thriller *Quai des Orfèvres*, towards his suspense shockers, *Le Salaire de la Peur* and *Les Diaboliques*, in which dynamite-laden lorries lurched over corrugated roads and murder victims returned to haunt their killers. André Cayatte, who took over a Prévert script to make *Les Amants de Vérone*, in the romantic–fatalist tradition, and then established himself as the director of 'lawyer's films', an advocate who (in a *Nous sommes tous des Assassins*) made the cinema a court-room and put the audience simultaneously into the dock and the jury-box.

All these film-makers remain active, and in varying degrees successful, yet none of them has added substantially to the reputations they had formed ten years or more ago. (This is just as true of many middle-generation film-makers in America and in Britain: one should not underestimate the difficulties of their calling.) It was against the Clouzots and Cléments that the young French critics, the future New Wave directors, railed so fiercely, making the word 'quality' a pejorative adjective and lashing out at films which seemed to them over-weight, over-stretched, and over-tired. The film which does a sound job within the limits of the fashionable formula is enough of an achievement to demand respect: the trouble is that the formulas change while the talent remains static, or goes through all sorts of antics in an effort to keep up. And it is certainly difficult to feel much excitement about films like Clouzot's *La Vérité*, with its court-room and flashbacks and Brigitte Bardot in suicidal agonies, or about Clément's Italian-based thriller *Plein Soleil*, or Cayatte's well-intentioned and sober *Le Passage du Rhin*. Under fire from their juniors, the film-makers fall back on prepared positions, with the box-office as the last line of defence.

Names among the missing, from any cinéaste's list of the major French film-makers of the early fifties, include Max Ophuls, Jacques Becker, and Jean Grémillon, all now dead, and Jean Cocteau, who always came to the cinema as a visitor rather than a resident, and scrawled his elegant epitaph to his screen career in *Le Testament d'Orphée*.

Max Ophuls was not a Frenchman; he was, in fact, the complete cosmopolitan, with a pre-war career of film-making in Germany, Italy, and France, followed by a spell in Hollywood which yielded *Letter from an Unknown Woman* and *The Reckless Moment*. When he settled in France, it was as a director to whom the label 'sophisticated' automatically and perhaps in the long run rather damagingly attached itself. People expected Ophuls to live up to some phantom vision of pre-war Vienna; and as a rule he was ready to oblige. His French films, *La Ronde*, that ring-a-roses game of elegant seduction, *Le Plaisir*, from a trio of de Maupassant stories, *Madame de . . .*, and *Lola Montès*, showed him also as a passionately decorative artist, one who behaved, as Peter Ustinov wrote in an obituary notice, 'like a watchmaker intent on making the smallest watch in the world and then, with a sudden flash of perversity, putting it up on a cathedral'.

Ophuls's stylistic trademark was the tracking shot: incessantly, flowingly, gracefully, his camera moved across and around the sets on which he expended so much care, from Madame de's dressing-room to the circus-ring of *Lola Montès*. And in fact this last film, which gave him CinemaScope and colour and followed Lola Montès's career backwards and sideways from the American circus of her final humiliation (with Peter Ustinov as ring-master) to the affairs with kings and composers, had the scale – the baroque frontage – to support the rococo of its intensely mannered style. But trouble with the film's backers, who wanted the opulence but not the intertwining of past and present, led to the release of a simplified version. And, in the middle of these arguments, the director died. In a quiet way, Ophuls had been an uncompromising film-maker; he wanted elegance, and more elegance, and the finest sets and the right to keep that camera endlessly moving; and beneath everything that made him the cinema's supreme interior decorator, he retained the cynical sentimentalism of an older Europe.

Jacques Becker took over a subject Ophuls was to have filmed in *Montparnasse 19*, a study of Modigliani. But Becker's precision talent was of a different order from Ophuls's: he described himself once as 'a bit of an entomologist', and his interest lay not in manufacturing the watch but in keeping an eye on the machinery. He retained something elusive about him, a sense of talent never employed for long at full stretch. He made happy comedies about Paris (*Antoine et Antoinette*, *Édouard et Caroline*), found himself with nothing very much to say about Left Bank youth (*Rendezvous de Juillet*), and wandered with Fernandel into an *Ali Baba*. In two films – *Casque d'or*, about the apaches and their girls of late nineteenth-century Paris, and his last picture, *Le Trou*, a study of men in prison – one felt that one was getting closest to the essential Becker, the man for whom cinema meant the re-creation of some specific moment in time, of the way people look and feel when involved in some action. The slogging, meticulous work of digging a hole in the floor of a prison cell; the way a warder methodically, impersonally, chops up every item in a prisoner's food parcel; the river party in *Casque d'or*, with its painterly echoes, and the moment in the same film when the lovers wake up in their country cottage: here Becker had his subject wholly pinned down. At other times, in other films, it seemed to slip away from him, and one retained the sense of a sympathetic voice muffled by hesitancies about precisely what was to be said.

Such uncertainties as can be sensed in Becker's career (and even more in that of Jean Grémillon, a film-maker of perversely unequal achievement) reflect perhaps the larger hesitations of the French industry during the middle fifties. At the beginning of the decade the top prizes at the Cannes and Venice festivals had been falling into the reliable hands of the Cléments and the Clouzots. A few years later France's share in the Grand Prix stakes had dwindled, and it was left to a documentarist such as Jacques-Yves Cousteau to take, with his underwater cameras, the honours that the feature industry could no longer command. The cycles had worked themselves out: Simone Signoret had played too many prostitutes, Christian-Jaque had put his wife, Martine Carol, through too many costume-pieces, Jean Gabin had sauntered down too many night streets.

There remained the three majestic, intolerable individualists, Cocteau, Jacques Tati, and Robert Bresson, making films on their own intransigent terms, not looking out, as any commercial director to some extent must, towards the audience, but inviting spectators into their own worlds. Cocteau let other people direct for or with him (Jean Delannoy made *L'Éternel Retour* and Clément worked on *La Belle et la Bête*; Jean-Pierre Melville, later the mentor of the *nouvelle vague*, made *Les Enfants terribles*); he put his own signature to Tristan and Isolde and Beauty and the Beast; he made a piercingly accurate piece of filmed theatre, as precise as a stop-watch, in *Les Parents terribles*. Then in 1950 came *Orphée* and a decade later its postscript, *Le Testament d'Orphée*.

Yet if Cocteau was absent during the fifties, engaged elsewhere after those few years of passionate attachment to the cinema, he had made in *Orphée* a film which was to haunt France's younger directors, as well as achieving that entirely personal screen poetry which his other fantasies had only reached after. In *Orphée* Cocteau is the master of his effects: the dissolving mirrors, through which the Princess passes to her underworld kingdom; the radio code messages ('*L'oiseau chante avec ses doigts*'); the motor-cyclists as agents of destruction, goggled and helmeted outriders of death. But this study of poetic obsession, of the artist in love with death and the lure of her unknown and shadowy kingdom, is hardly the hermetic and sealed-off work that some writers considered it. Time has confirmed its relevance.

The fatiguing lack of stability today [wrote Gavin Lambert in a review] pushes the artist further away from humanity, from common sympathies – pushes him towards the mirrors of infinitely strange reflections, to a feverish search for new and elusive revelations, oscillates him between the world of everyday realities and a land of private longings and apprehensions.

Cocteau reaches from the mirrors of *Orphée* to the mirrors of *L'Année dernière à Marienbad*; from its code messages to those of *Paris nous appartient*.

The French critics have often found it profitable to compare Jacques Tati and Robert Bresson: austere comedian and cinema theologian, autocrats of the screen who ignore, for whatever different purposes, all the accepted rules of timing and emphasis. Tati's comic paraphernalia – the stick and the raincoat and the stiff, loping, oddly top-heavy walk – encase a fundamentally serious man, who seems to have chosen silence to emphasize his own isolation. Tati can throw a factory into chaos (as in *Mon Oncle*) and remain uninvolved: he is off somewhere studying the mathematical formula of a joke. Genial but remote, his Monsieur Hulot is always trying to bridge the gap between himself and other people, sending out messages which remain unanswered, grappling with problems which, he gloomily recognizes, would have been the better left untried. The comic tension is in this conflict between what Hulot wants and what he has: Tati, unlike Chaplin, does not take sides with his *alter ego*.

If Tati is the mathematician of comedy, Bresson is the geometrician of the dramatic cinema. Gradually, he has evolved his own austere and rather terrifying methods. Early in the war he was acting as assistant to René Clair, in retrospect an improbable but not entirely unfitting alliance, on a picture which had to be left unfinished. He set *Les Anges du Péché* in a convent; he made the astonishing *Les Dames du Bois de Boulogne* from a Cocteau adaptation of an eighteenth-century novel. Then, with

Journal d'un Curé de Campagne, Un Condamné à mort s'est échappé, Pickpocket, and *Procès de Jeanne d'Arc,* he mapped his own world, that cold place where his characters fight their lonely battles for belief.

Since his early films, Bresson has rejected the professional actor; he had in fact, by the time of *Pickpocket,* rejected 'acting' in any conventional sense. His characters – the pain-wracked young priest in *Journal,* the wartime prisoner in *Un Condamné,* the thief of *Pickpocket,* St Joan herself – are engaged in a spiritual adventure; and even the escape from prison, with its quiet exultation of release, is first and foremost a conquest of the spirit. All these films are stripped down, concentrated, the details of background and setting (the dimensions of a prison cell; the precise techniques of a pickpocket) observed with extreme intensity. All of them have to do with faith, or rather the state of grace. The pickpocket, pursuing his compulsive career of theft through the Métro stations of Paris, is a mysterious, almost anonymous sinner, a hunted man who can be saved only by attaining this condition of grace. For Bresson, the drama that counts is always the interior one, which is why he keeps away from the associations that the professional actor brings with him, finds his own players and drills them into a total subordination to his will. He is the most unrelenting of contemporary film-makers; at his most implacably Bressonian (as in *Pickpocket*) one of the most difficult. His actors wear the Bresson face, haunted and enigmatic; he takes them on a series of spiritual journeys without signposts; he makes nothing easy, for us or for himself. Driving himself, his characters, his audience, he imposes his view of where man stands in relation to God: a Bresson film is an exercise of will, in which the only victory is in surrender.

7. The Free French

By comparison with painting or the novel film-making inevitably seems an art of compromise, both because it must be to some extent a collective adventure, not a one-man show, and because the cinema, whether we like it or not, remains an art that needs an audience. A novelist can sell a few thousand copies of a book and leave his publisher tolerably satisfied; a feature film, however economically made, must be seen by a few hundred thousand people at least if its backers are to recover their investment. And the film must be seen *now*: the lost masterpiece, the work so far ahead of its time that its appeal remains restricted to a closed circle, is likely in this transitory and relentless art to stay lost. Yet the artist, unless he has the luck to be equipped with a naturally commercial talent – and why not, since the idea that art must be difficult, obscure, and solitary has been one of the more depressing legends of our time – will still try to gain for himself something of the novelist's independence. Not without difficulty, and periods of inactivity and uncertainty, film-makers as dissimilar as Bresson and Antonioni and Satyajit Ray have come within striking distance of attaining it. The growing audience for the so-called minority film has made the going that much easier.

Yet the idea of the film-maker as novelist remains something of an illusion, if only because of the conditions of the craft itself. If the critic traditionally writes in terms of the director and the scriptwriter, he is none the less aware that between the conception and the creation stand the technicians, the publicists, the businessmen; that an effect may be achieved because of, or in spite of, the director who will be credited with it. But the French have always accorded the director that respect which Hollywood, more realistically in its own terms, tends to reserve for the producer. And in France during the fifties the conception of the 'written' film ('*l'écriture*', in Bresson's phrase) turned up more and more frequently in critical discussion.

Alexandre Astruc, a critic who was himself to become a film-maker, wrote a celebrated article called 'Le Caméra Stylo' as early as 1948. In it he said:

The cinema . . . becomes bit by bit a language. By a language I mean the form in which and through which an artist can express his thoughts, however abstract they may be, or translate his obsessions, *just as in an essay or a novel* [my italics]. . . . The film will gradually free itself from the tyranny of the visual, of the image for its own sake, of the immediate and concrete anecdote, to become a means of writing as supple and subtle as the written word. . . . What interests us in the cinema today is the creation of this language.

The camera with which one writes: this, as Astruc formulated it in his article, was an ideal towards which the cinema was reaching, and the ideal envisaged the film as essentially an expression of a single point of view. This kind of theorizing might, at another time and in another place, have remained simply a critic's conception. But by the late fifties, by which time Astruc himself was directing, and Roger Vadim had found Brigitte Bardot and given the international cinema a new star and a new dream, and the French industry some blazing commercial successes, France's cinema was ripe for change.

An official spokesman, M. Jacques Flaud, then director of the Centre Nationale de la Cinématographie, urged the industry to pursue a conscious policy of risk. 'If producers are unwilling to give opportunities to young directors,' he said, 'if they prefer to trust to "sure things" . . . if a director tries more for profit than for his own development, then the French cinema will mark time and stiffen up.' The hardening of the arteries looked to be setting in, and must be resisted. Whether or not M. Flaud's exhortations produced any direct results, French producers had been learning the same hard lessons as the English and the Americans: 'sure things' were sure no longer, public taste had become fickle, unpredictable, and uncertain.

Before the producers could demonstrate any readiness to invest in youth, however, the young directors had to present themselves. In Britain, at about the same time, most of the creative drive and excitement was channelled into the theatre, with the Royal Court playwrights leading the way. In France, the same kind of rebellious energy could be harnessed by the movies. Cinema was fashionable, and more than fashionable. To the young audiences which attended the Cinémathèque Française's film-shows it was a passion; and the magazine *Cahiers du Cinéma*, from which so many of the young film-makers came, formulated critical theories which were to be the effective springboard for the *nouvelle vague*.

The influence of *Cahiers du Cinéma* extends far beyond its comparatively modest circulation. It has set the world of film criticism by the ears, recruiting disciples, compelling opponents to think again about their own terms of reference. Dissenters may find the *Cahiers* line a matter of extreme enthusiasms linked to tenuous theories; but even in disagreement they may come closer to an understanding of how the cinema works. The issue, too, is not just an abstract one of critical attitudes, since the film-makers who wrote for the magazine (François Truffaut, Jean-Luc Godard, Claude Chabrol, Jacques Doniol-Valcroze, and Eric Rohmer, among others) have naturally pursued in their own work the ideas they advocated as critics.

This magazine has been identified with two main viewpoints. First, an insistence that what really counts in cinema is the '*mise en scène*' (a term which virtually defies translation, meaning something more than direction and perhaps most easily expressed as the creation of mood and ambiance); and secondly, the so-called '*politique des auteurs*'. Every critic, to put it naïvely, responds more readily to some film-makers than to others: *Cahiers* made out of these admirations a deliberate policy, so that directors approved by the magazine could do almost nothing wrong, and directors vetoed could do very little right. Among the admired were Hitchcock, Fritz Lang, Otto Preminger, Nicholas Ray, Anthony Mann, the Italian Vittorio Cottafavi. Instructed that 'Losey, Lang, Preminger, and Cottafavi are the greatest of the great', or that 'to remain insensitive to the thousand beauties of Nicholas Ray's *Party Girl* is to turn one's back resolutely on the modern cinema', readers brought up to more orthodox conventions were liable to feel that critical values had been stood firmly on their heads. This is just what the *Cahiers* writers set out to do. Critics, they claimed, had been making it too easy for the de Sicas and the Satyajit Rays because they paid too much attention to the humanist theme, put content before style. But *mise en scène* ('a certain way of extending the *élans* of the soul in the movements of the body', to quote Astruc) takes no account of a film's subject.

Behind and through the extravagant language, the often perverse enthusiasms, the tracking down of meanings never dreamt of by the film-makers themselves, a passion for cinema blazes. French 'quality' movie-making is derided; American directors are exalted (and undoubtedly these young critics have been sustained by a pleasingly romantic view of America, the easier to keep up in that the revealing niceties of dialogue, all too apparent to English ears, may sometimes pass them by). The magazine was staffed by potential directors, journalists by default. Given their chance, they erupted into action.

In fact, at the outset, some of them made their own chances. Young film-makers spent their own money, or their wives', or their parents'; friends helped each other; film stock and equipment were borrowed. Working on a near-amateur basis, or fairly cheaply within the industry, they made some films (Claude Chabrol's *Le Beau Serge*, Louis Malle's *L'Ascenseur pour l'Échafaud*). Then, at the Cannes Festival of 1959, the filmgoing world awoke to the realization that a whole new generation of film-makers had declared itself. Marcel Camus's *Orfeu Negro* took the festival Grand Prix; François Truffaut's *Les Quatre Cents Coups* the prize for direction; Alain Resnais's *Hiroshima mon Amour* the International Critics' Prize. Within a matter of months, the expression *nouvelle vague* (a journalist's invention and about as meaningless, in itself, as 'Angry Young Man') was turning up everywhere.

Anyone who did anything at all in the French cinema was liable to find himself labelled 'New Wave'. In fact, the three Cannes prizes were indicative. Marcel Camus, already in his middle forties, had been working for years as an assistant director; Alain Resnais, in his late thirties, was one of France's best-known directors of short films; François Truffaut, still in his twenties, came from criticism and *Cahiers*. France's state-aid system, with its encouragement of quality production in shorts and documentaries, helped young directors to find the experience they needed before embarking on a feature; but not all the newcomers were ex-critics, and not all of them were young. Many had been waiting years for the kind of opportunities now offered. And these opportunities? Enough to say that in 1959 twenty-four directors made their first feature films, and in 1960 a further forty-three.

Ever since the film industries of the world became commercially organized, there had been nothing quite like this: when one considers the sheer size of the production investment involved, it is sufficiently easy to see why. But producers, naturally, were acting out of shrewder motives than a philanthropic devotion to young talent. Some early New Wave films (Claude Chabrol's *Les Cousins*, Godard's *À Bout de Souffle*) were outstanding commercial successes. If youth could make profits, youth could win backing; and in the highly speculative atmosphere of modern film-making, the bigger the gamble, perhaps, the bigger the opportunity. Rather than make one expensive film, with all the correct box-office insurance in the way of story and star casting, and see the whole thing go down the drain, a producer might prefer to put the same kind of money into three or four cheap films by young directors, gambling that at least one of them would prove another *Les Cousins*.

In the long run, and for a number of reasons, the gamble failed to pay off financially. By the end of 1961, François Truffaut, questioned about the 'hostile attitude of the distributors towards the work of young film-makers', agreed that there was 'a good deal of mistrust' and found it not unreasonable. 'No new-wave film,' he said, 'has been a real financial success for more than eighteen months.' (He included his own *Tirez sur le Pianiste*.) Businessmen, in these circumstances, were entitled to walk warily.

What had the new directors wanted? In Truffaut's words:

Films used to be impersonal because of constraints : use of foreign actors, too many screenwriters, distributors' pressures, top-heavy technical crews, extravagant budgets. We thought it should be possible to simplify all this by working freely and making cheap films on simple subjects. A whole collection of new-wave pictures are alike only in what they reject: no extras, no theatrical intrigues, no expensive sets, no explanatory scenes. . . . What makes it confusing is that the qualities of this new cinema – grace, lightness, modesty, elegance, speed – are paralleled by its failings: frivolity, lack of conscience, *naïveté*. . . .

Anyone can now make a film, they sweepingly said: the problem has become not the first film but the second one. In the limited sense in which this 'anyone' was true, this meant that young directors had the chances no highly organized modern film industry had ever been able to afford them. But, inevitably, relatively few of the hundred or more new film-makers who turned up between 1958 and 1961 could find the talent or the stamina to support their own enthusiasm. In this climate of chaotic excitement and opportunity, people wanted not so much to make films about anything in particular as simply to make films, to go out and show that they could do it too. One movie fed on another; a producer who had struck it rich with one picture shopped for something which would achieve that entrepreneur's impossible dream of somehow looking different but exactly the same. Young film-makers made movies about themselves, and about their friends, who were also film-makers, and about other movies. In the public mind, some sort of composite image began to build up. The film would feature a group of young people, vaguely well-off or at least not much concerned with the problems of earning a living; they would sit around talking; they would go to the cinema and talk about that; they would drive off in their white Triumphs and Sunbeams for a high-speed sequence on the roads around Paris; the love-scenes would get the film a British 'X' certificate; someone would probably be killed; and in the background there would be a cool jazz score or an assertive piece of classical music. If the film came from within the inner circle, a copy of *Cahiers du Cinéma* might somewhere be flourished, or one of the *nouvelle vague* directors would put in a friendly appearance in the cast.

This image, which has no real relation to the films of Resnais or Truffaut or Demy, or half a dozen of the more durable talents, undoubtedly proved a commercial liability. In box-office terms, audiences in France showed a decisive preference for a film like Clouzot's *La Vérité*, which invited them to be agreeably horrified by Brigitte Bardot as a sluttish young rebel, rather than for the new-wave anarchy, which did not concern itself about what they thought. The French public, like any other, prefers to be given some kind of moral yardstick; and the new directors rounded on bourgeois morality as they did on bourgeois traditions of film-making.

Jean-Luc Godard's *À Bout de Souffle* spoke out in the strident voice of arrogant, assured, and very considerable young talent: it was the kind of first film which announces the arrival of someone who really will look at film-making in a new way. In this study of a young amateur gangster and the American girl who takes up with and ultimately betrays him, one gets almost a distilled essence of the *nouvelle vague* production. The film can be called amoral, because morality hardly enters the question; the characters are circling warily around each other, experts in self-mockery as in self-doubt, tentative explorers of their own personalities. They do not know quite where or what they are; and Godard does not want the audience to be too confident of its own whereabouts. If you think you have heard a pistol shot, it will turn out to be nothing more violent than a clash of car bumpers; and the film is edited so that the traditional time sequence is broken, with jump cuts (by which we may see the beginning and the end of an action, but not the bit in the middle), with repeated shifts of place and viewpoint. In the conventional film, if you are moving to a new setting – a scene as simple, say, as a couple talking in a room – you probably begin with an establishing shot, so that the audience sees the room and gets its bearings. The new directors are as likely as not to begin on the close-up; and when the camera does pull back from the faces to show us where we are, it very probably is not where we expected.

Although an over-simplified example, this is not an untypical one, and such gambits are not merely stylistic fancy-work. They underline an attitude to film-making. If the director's basic concern is to tell a story to a large audience, he will help the spectator to follow it easily: if a character tells us that he is going to do something, and there is then a cut, we are conditioned to expect that in the next scene he will be doing the thing he talked about. But if the film-maker is concerned not so much with a story as with the immediate instant, with the involvement of the audience less in a narrative than a sensation or an experience, with the kind of chances and hazards that intervene in life, then these wires of convention can be cut and left dangling. The film finds and imposes its own logic.

What we see is what the director chooses to show us: if he finds something boring and decides to skip over it, with an implied 'etc., etc.', then he assumes that we know enough about cinema conventions to keep up with him. In *À Bout de Souffle*, certainly, the characters themselves have no existence outside the context in which Godard evokes them: Jean Seberg, the American girl, at once the dream and the betrayer, and Jean-Paul Belmondo, the would-be Humphrey Bogart. The film itself is the thing; and the audience finds at least part of its pleasure in a sharing of the director's own excitement, the sense of glee he transparently feels at the improvised moment that sets the screen alight, the experiments with timing, the investigation of a language. Godard's second feature, *Le Petit Soldat*, was banned for political reasons; his third, *Une Femme est une Femme*, brimmed over with jokes and spoofs, snatches of improvisation, and loving pastiches of Hollywood musicals. Exhilarating, and in the long run exhausting, it served as a kind of exhibitionist demonstration that a film is a film is a film.

But all this higher gamesmanship, in *Une Femme est une Femme* or in Truffaut's *Tirez sur le Pianiste*, leads somewhere. In Godard's case, to *Vivre sa Vie*, a film about a prostitute (or perhaps, more accurately, about a girl who happens to be a prostitute) made with a kind of desperate purity. Out of exhibitionism comes a daring austerity, the random power controlled and put to a very precise purpose; and, still, we are insistently reminded that what we are watching is a *film*, and nothing else.

In a picture such as Jacques Demy's *Lola*, with its lyrical camerawork, its elegant variations on the theme of love lost, love found, love rejected, the references to other films and film-makers (a slow-motion scene, for instance, which pays explicit tribute to Jean Vigo) are beautifully integrated. But the director must have found his own style before he can hope to juggle effectively with these reminiscences of other people. Godard and Demy have quoted with style, where other film-makers slide into easy affectation. Chabrol's *À Double Tour*, for instance, shows off the director's admiration for Hitchcock; Louis Malle's *Vie privée* provides a whole compendium of tricks, allusions, bits of cinematic poker-work. This generation of directors, born of the cinema, have their references so thoroughly at their fingertips that some of their work could almost stand annotation for the benefit of the uninitiated.

The French cinema has been influenced by existentialism (inevitably) and by the *nouveau roman*, the novels of writers such as Alain Robbe-Grillet, Michel Butor, or Nathalie Sarraute who have set out to anatomize an experience and who deliberately choose to play down rather than to play up, to keep to a single angle of vision, to leave their readers with half their questions unanswered. Of course, the *nouveau roman* also admits the influence of the cinema. Both have been working towards an 'art of appearances', concentrating on how things look and feel to the eye of the beholder, leaving us to make up our own minds about the points they refuse to answer. What looks like a mountain may be a molehill in reality. The significant thing is that we see it as a mountain; and from where, in any case, do we take our notion of 'objective' reality? The results have inevitably been called nihilist. They have also been called neo-Fascist. Of *Le*

Petit Soldat, the French critic Jacques Siclier has written: 'Political theories of right and left are meaningless, as are moral and social values . . . there exists no other ideal than the *acte gratuit*.' In the France of the long Algerian war, the threats of a military *putsch*, the armoured cars standing guard in the streets of Paris, the France of inflation and political murder, the artist's response was to make emphatically plain his own withdrawal.

The moral or social judgement, however, is precisely the one this cinema discounts: it leaves us to our own morality. Why, Truffaut has been asked, does he reject the social subject? 'There are half a dozen Communist film-makers in France,' he has answered, 'and about fifteen left-wingers. Leave such themes to them.' Irresponsible, or honest, or both? While the young English film-makers were debating commitment, the French were admitting their open infatuation with the cinema. But after the deliberate gesture of disengagement, the retreat into private worlds, they are inclined to come back looking very much like humanists.

Truffaut, quite possibly the most talented and almost certainly the most sympathetic of the young French directors, came close to making this retreat with his second film. The powerfully autobiographic *Les Quatre Cents Coups*, about a boy searching for his place in an unfriendly world, was the most openly engaged of the early *nouvelle vague* films. Its final image, when the child runs away to the sea and the last shot of the picture freezes into his long, silent, questioning stare out at the audience, remains one of the most directly haunting in contemporary cinema. Truffaut, clearly, had given us a large part of himself; and the style he adopted, part lyrical, part (such as the psychiatrist's examination) documentary and clinical, was itself imposed by his theme. But he felt, he has said, that the film passed out of his hands once the big international audience took it up. And so, in *Tirez sur le Pianiste*, he made something to please himself, a mixture of comedy and pathos, echoes of the American B-picture, charm and impudence, a film about the loneliness of a man for whom life has become too difficult, but also a celebration of its maker's long love-affair with the cinema. *Jules et Jim* continued the love-affair. Truffaut speeds up action, freezes shots, sends his camera in great swooping arcs across the countryside, cuts in old newsreels of the First World War, and creates a style so zestful that the film becomes touched with the magic of its director's intoxication. He has the gift of making film-making look wonderfully easy, like a man running down a long, sunlit road with a camera in his hand. And along with this enchantment goes a nostalgia for innocence: he seems always to be glancing back over his shoulder, trying to catch unawares that wonderful moment, if it ever existed, when life seemed all gaiety and ease. Like Renoir, his acknowledged mentor, Truffaut makes films about friendship.

If critical breezes have wafted about the heads of Truffaut and Godard, they have lashed at Alain Resnais, a director from a slightly older generation, even if his first feature was made at approximately the same time, and one who thinks in terms much more obviously 'literary' than his younger colleagues. Neither *Hiroshima mon Amour* nor *L'Année dernière à Marienbad*, it seems, can be watched with anything approaching equanimity. And the tone of the criticism – *Hiroshima* being labelled 'a woman's picture', that unkindest cut of all; *Marienbad* seen as an elaborate maze with nothing whatsoever at its centre – carries an unusual edge of resentment. One might think, from the way Resnais's films have been assailed by some reviewers, that his kind of film-making threatened some powerful take-over bid for the cinema.

In fact, Resnais occupies rather an isolated position; and the technique of his films, which owes more than that of most modern directors to editing, an extremely subtle timing and relationship of shots, does not particularly encourage imitation.

Resnais came to features via shorts, notably the art documentaries (*Van Gogh*, *Guernica*) with which he began; and in everything he has done since then there have been elements of the art film. *Marienbad* has been described as a film about a statue – literally and metaphorically. But the director's later documentaries (*Toute la Mémoire du Monde*, about the Bibliothèque Nationale; *Nuit et Brouillard*, which fused the desolation of the relics of Auschwitz with the horrors of its past) indicated just as clearly the course he was to take.

Both these shorts, and both his first two features, have to do with time and memory: the library which stores up the past; the concentration camp which still lives on, and whose horrors cannot be extinguished because they are over; the relationship between a girl haunted by a wartime tragedy and a city haunted by the war's greatest agony; the efforts by which a man tries to persuade a woman that a dream (or is it a dream?) can take on reality. On the features, Resnais worked in the closest collaboration with two writers, Marguerite Duras and Alain Robbe-Grillet, themselves magnets for controversy. Mme Duras's heroine (in *Hiroshima*) has an instinct for self-dramatization; she lives on and through her emotions; she has 'seen nothing in Hiroshima', yet she has made of her time there a catalytic experience, compelling her to relive her past. Out of this reliving, or, rather, this fusion of two experiences, achieved through some of the most imaginative editing in cinema history, Resnais made a Proustian reconnaissance, time present and time past brought together in the series of juxtapositions, Hiroshima–Nevers.

L'Année dernière à Marienbad moved much further into subjectivity: here the audience is not responding to a lived experience but being subjected to the persuasive force of a conviction. In a great baroque hotel, all icy corridors and cold statuary, a man and a woman meet. Their relationship has the quality of a dream, since in this film time has no objective existence. Everything may have happened before, or at this moment, or never; we can make what we want of it, surrendering to the hypnotic pull of Resnais's imagery or rejecting it. Reality is equated with possibility: the images collide and overlap, recur and disintegrate, and the film constructs its own line of continuity through the emotional echoes they set reverberating.

The film makes a closed circle, a closed experience – *L'Année dernière* or Persuasion, as Resnais has called it. What are the characters doing when they are not in that fantastic hotel? Nothing, says Robbe-Grillet: they have no existence other than the one we have given them. And we are back with the conception of the film as an end in itself, which has perhaps marked the *nouvelle vague*'s closest approach to a theory. Resnais the formalist, the literary man, Godard the improviser, the 'pure' filmmaker, stand at opposite extremes. But both have turned their backs on a cinema of naturalism or direct narrative: the *film d'auteur* becomes an autonomous creation, a self-sufficient entity.

It is impossible, happily, to pin down a *nouvelle vague* style, because in a sense there never was a *nouvelle vague*, but simply a coming together of an extraordinary number of talented people in one national industry at one time. Henri Colpi, editor of Resnais's films, director of *Une Aussi Longue Absence*, a film of sensibility if a little inclined to wallow in its own hyper-sensitivity; Alexandre Astruc, the former critic, influenced by Antonioni (notably in *La Proie pour l'Ombre*) and another very conscious stylist; Philippe de Broca, a comedy director with a fine sense of the absurd in decoration; Jacques Rivette, whose *Paris nous appartient* created a disturbing vision of life in an age of anxiety, of the neurosis which feeds on its own fears; Claude Chabrol, the trend-setter; Agnès Varda, of *Cléo de 5 à 7*; Chris Marker, most idiosyncratic of documentary directors … the long line of talent pays out. What brought them together, however, was nothing more substantial than opportunity. Now that the *nouvelle vague* is already a thing of the past, the commentators move in to sort out the various groups and attitudes, from the *Cahiers* directors (the sort of people, one French critic has said, who discovered Shakespeare by way of Orson Welles) to the artists obviously concerned to bridge the gap between film and novel.

Since the Cannes victory of 1959, France's cinema has been more or less dominated, creatively if not commercially, by its young directors. Two exceptionally talented cameramen, Raoul Coutard and Henri Decae, have come with them to give many of the best of these films their distinctive look; and the hand-held camera has become a kind of badge of honour for the improvised film. Yet this generation has not, on the whole, managed to conquer the French public, and the situation in France poses one of the basic dilemmas of the contemporary cinema. As the big commercial film becomes more impersonal, less a matter of one man's creative idea than of logistics and box-office strategy, so the rebel artist is liable, as a natural reaction, to cut himself off. If the mass medium rejects him, then he rejects the mass medium. Ironically, Truffaut has complained that *Les Quatre Cents Coups* was seen by too many people and *Tirez sur le Pianiste* by too few: illogical and cantankerous though this may seem, it is also a perfectly understandable expression of the artist's wish to find a public, and his fear that if he does find a really big one it will be at some sacrifice of himself. The French directors know that their kind of individualism in the cinema is bought at the price of making films cheaply; and, meanwhile, they watch the queues on the boulevards for *The Longest Day* and *How the West Was Won* and *Ben-Hur* – the films that are helping to keep an industry solvent. So precarious, indeed, is the whole balance of modern cinema that France's own industry, which in 1959–60 invested freely in talent, found itself in 1963 hovering on the edge of a production strike.

8. Room at the Top

Is there a British new wave, and if not, why not? The question has been repeatedly asked, and answered in terms of organization (the difficulty of raising financial backing; the even greater problems of obtaining distribution) and more curtly in terms of national attitudes of mind (the British have the wrong approach to the cinema). In France, a brief period of unprecedented opportunity coincided with a surge of creative energy. In Britain we have not yet had the opportunity, and without it there is no way of telling whether we have the talent. But we do, unmistakably, have a new cinema after our own fashion; and if it looks entirely different from the one across the Channel, and never more so than when striving most arduously to copy it, this is because the formative influences have had so very little in common.

'Britain's cinema is the most conformist in the world,' said the Soviet director Sergei Youtkevich, when French journalists had been challenging him on *Soviet* stolidity. If this were true – and on questions of conformism the Russians certainly have a claim to be regarded as experts – there would be reasons, of a sort, to account for it. The collective memory of the British film industry is haunted by crises of one kind and another, so that the trade unions have been notably chary, despite television's aid to employment, about relaxing their regulations to make the going a little easier for anyone trying to produce films on the cheap. Where some of the *nouvelle vague* directors made films initially for £30,000 or so, a *Saturday Night and Sunday Morning* must go well over the £100,000 mark. In France, with union regulations much less firmly enforced, the director and cameraman really could do the thing more or less on their own, at least to the extent of shooting a sequence in fairly casual conditions. Here, union rules about the number of men required to handle each piece of equipment are strictly laid down and obeyed. British directors must work, of necessity as well as by choice, within the industry system; even if they had £30,000 or £40,000 of their own money to play with, there would be little point in sinking it in a film which, owing to the effective control of the main distribution channels by the Rank and A.B.C. circuits, might well remain virtually unseen if it did not fit into the accepted commercial framework.

More telling than this, however, are all the imponderables of a national attitude. In this country, the best creative talent has generally fought a little shy of the cinema; successive governments have provided aid but have not measured it, as have so many European countries, by any qualitative standards; and there have been fewer people concerned to discuss movies seriously, other than as a potential contributor to juvenile delinquency. More, perhaps, than any other industry in Western Europe, Britain's remains dominated by a view of the cinema as an entertainment business first, last, and all the time. Other industries may be run by robber barons or flamboyant impresarios. Britain's has its accountants – and, again, an inconvenient memory of the kind of debt one impresario, Korda, left behind him. In any case, the big companies which control British cinema are thoroughly diversified. If films no longer exercise the pull they once did, there will always remain the

1a. Luchino Visconti's *La Terra Trema*

1b. Vittorio de Sica's *Miracle in Milan*

2. Roberto Rossellini's *Francesco, Giullare di Dio*

Italy

3a. Alain Delon and Monica Vitti in Michelangelo Antonioni's *The Eclipse*

3b. Françoise Prévost, Dino Mele, and Umberto Orsini in Giuseppe Patroni Griffi's *Il Mare*. (Antonioni's influence on younger Italian directors is evident from this still)

Italy

4a. Marcello Mastroianni in the final beach sequence of Federico Fellini's *La Dolce Vita*

4b. The boy in Ermanno Olmi's *Il Posto*

5. Preparing to shoot the last sequence of *L'Avventura*, with Monica Vitti and Gabriele Ferzetti on the hotel terrace

6a. Franco Citti in Pier Paolo Pasolini's *Accattone*

6b. Italian spectacle: Vittorio Cottafavi's *Hercules Conquers Atlantis*

7a. Lauren Bacall and Humphrey Bogart in Howard Hawks's *The Big Sleep*

7b. Judy Garland sings in a scene from George Cukor's *A Star is Born*

8a. James Dean and Burl Ives in Elia Kazan's *East of Eden*

8b. Celeste Holm, Hugh Marlowe, Bette Davis, and Anne Baxter in Joseph Mankiewicz's *All About Eve*

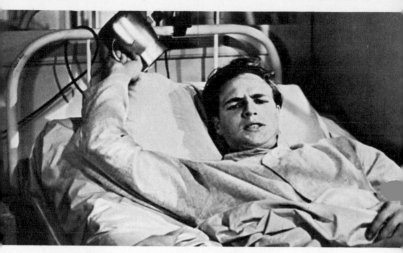

9a. Marlon Brando as the crippled ex-soldier in Fred Zinnemann's *The Men*. (This, in 1950, was Brando's first screen appearance)

9b. Gloria Swanson and William Holden in Billy Wilder's *Sunset Boulevard*

U.S.A.

10a. Dan Dailey, Gene Kelly, and Michael Kidd in a number from *It's Always Fair Weather*, directed by Gene Kelly and Stanley Donen

10b. Peter Lorre, Marco Tulli, and Ivor Barnard form a characteristic group of John Huston plotters from *Beat the Devil*

11a. Elisha Cook Jun. and Marie Windsor in Stanley Kubrick's thriller *The Killing*

11b. Fred Astaire in a mock-gangster number from Vincente Minnelli's musical *The Band Wagon*

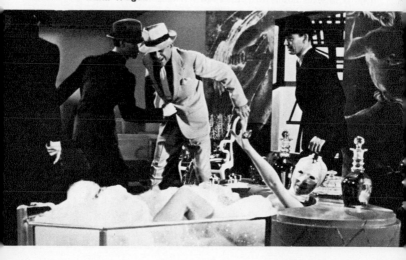

12a. A Chinese city constructed in Spain for Nicholas Ray's *55 Days at Peking*. The set was finally burnt down for the climax of the picture

12b. A pioneer family in John Ford's *Wagonmaster*

U.S.A.

13a. Ben Carruthers and Lelia Goldoni in John Cassavetes's *Shadows* (the new American cinema of improvisation)

13b. Alfred Hitchcock crossing the skyline in a scene from his own film *I Confess*

14a. Jean Renoir's *Le Déjeuner sur l'herbe*

14b. Peter Ustinov and Martine Carol in Max Ophuls's *Lola Montès*

15a. Édouard Dermithe and Maria Casarès in Jean Cocteau's *Orphée*

15b. Delphine Seyrig in Alain Resnais's *L'Année dernière à Marienbad*

16a. Claude Laydu in Robert Bresson's *Le Journal d'un curé de campagne*

16b. Gérard Philipe in René Clair's *Les Belles de nuit*

17a. Jeanne Moreau in François Truffaut's *Jules et Jim*

17b. The cameraman Raoul Coutard with Anouk Aimée on the set of *Lola*

18a. Brigitte Bardot in Roger Vadim's *Le Repos du guerrier*

18b. The last sequence of Jean-Luc Godard's *Vivre sa vie*: the shooting of Nana (Anna Karina)

19b. Laurence Harvey in Jack Clayton's *Room at the Top*

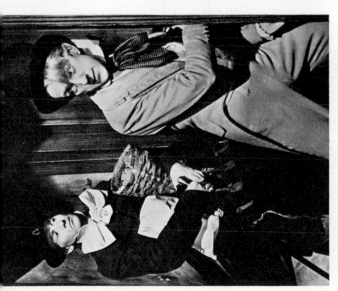

19a. John Mills and Alec Guinness in David Lean's *Great Expectations*

Great Britain

20a. Dennis Price and Valerie Hobson in Robert Hamer's *Kind Hearts and Coronets*

20b. Alec Guinness and Danny Green in Alexander Mackendrick's *The Ladykillers*

Great Britain

21a. Joseph Cotten in a Vienna street scene from Carol Reed's *The Third Man*

21b. Richard Harris and Rachel Roberts in Lindsay Anderson's *This Sporting Life*

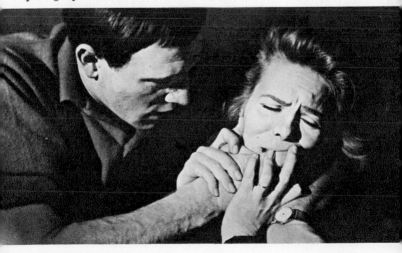

22. Edith Evans (Miss Weston) in Tony Richardson's *Tom Jones*

23a. A caricatured Churchill in *The Fall of Berlin*, from the height of the Stalinist period of Soviet film-making. (Director: Chiaureli)

23b. A scene from Sergei Samsonov's Chekhov adaptation, *The Grasshopper* (Soviet Union)

The Soviet Union and Poland

24a. The most popular Soviet film of recent years: Grigori Chukrai's *The Ballad of a Soldier*

24b. Roman Polanski's short, *Two Men and a Wardrobe* (Poland)

The Soviet Union and Poland

25a. Zbygniew Cybulski in *Ashes and Diamonds*, the third part of Andrzej Wajda's war trilogy (Poland)

25b. A scene from Wojciech Has's *Farewells* (Poland)

Japan and India

26a. Kenji Mizoguchi's *Sansho Dayu* (Japan)

26b. Yasujiro Ozu's *Early Autumn* (Japan)

Japan and India

27a. Akira Kurosawa's *The Lower Depths* (adapted from Gorky) with Toshiro Mifune (Japan)

27b. Satyajit Ray's *The World of Apu*: the return home of Apu with his wife (India)

28. Luis Buñuel's *Nazarin*

29. Leopoldo Torre Nilsson's *Fin de Fiesta*

30a. Ingmar Bergman's *Smiles of a Summer Night*, with Jarl Kulle, Gunnar Björnstrand, and Margit Carlquist

30b. Michael Cacoyannis's *Our Last Spring*

31a. Alf Sjöberg's *Miss Julie*, with Anita Björk

31b. Orson Welles's *The Trial*, adapted from Kafka, filmed in Paris and Yugoslavia

32a. Denis and Terry Sanders's *A Time Out of War*

32b. Georges Franju's *Hôtel des Invalides*

bowling alleys and the bingo games, or whatever follows them in the way of an entertainment fashion, to keep things going.

We must remember that we are, at best, a middle-aged industry [wrote the producer Carl Foreman in a letter to the film trade Press urging the foundation of a national film school]. We must ask ourselves who will be writing, directing, producing, acting in and otherwise contributing to British films ten years from now.

Others, looking across the Channel, have asked the same kind of questions. France and Italy have their defiantly young directors, as unafraid of making mistakes as they are of making pictures; and Britain's cinema by contrast looks scared of cutting loose, of appearing immature or juvenile. The mistakes it makes will be the enervating ones of cautious middle-age; its directors, if they have followed that time-honoured route from clapper-boy to film-maker, will have had some of the energy and snap knocked out of them by the time they get there.

Yet the British cinema unmistakably wears a face very different from the one of only a few years ago: it acquires a Tony Richardson (from the theatre), a Karel Reisz (from documentary), a Jack Clayton (from within the industry), a John Schlesinger (from television): it finds an Albert Finney or a Tom Courtenay or a Rita Tushingham to act for it. Three or four strands have come together, summed up, in however cursory a way, in the backgrounds of these directors.

One might begin, as with the French, with a magazine, although in this case the time-lag was a great deal longer and any detectable influence had been filtered through other channels. *Sequence*, founded in Oxford in 1947, with Lindsay Anderson as one of its co-editors, and later joined by Karel Reisz, took an argumentative line about the British cinema from the start, parading its intransigence with undergraduate confidence: 'The important question is whether spurious elements from hack commercial films are allowed like a virus to invade good ones and vitiate their success,' dogmatized Gavin Lambert in *Sequence Two*. 'If you enjoy *L'Éternel Retour* you may also enjoy *King Kong* but not *Black Narcissus*. If you enjoy *Black Narcissus* you cannot enjoy *L'Éternel Retour*. (If you think you enjoyed both, you are wrong),' hectored Lindsay Anderson in the same issue. It looked as though a Leavis had come to film criticism, and *Sequence* had enthusiasms to propagate as well as bravado. By the time it finally died the death of all little magazines, it had written its way into film history.

Lindsay Anderson and Karel Reisz moved on, in 1956, to 'Free Cinema', which again began partly as a movement of protest and dissatisfaction with things as they were. The first Free Cinema show – Anderson's *O Dreamland*, Karel Reisz and Tony Richardson's *Momma Don't Allow*, Lorenza Mazzetti's *Together* – packed the National Film Theatre. However limited the scale of the enterprise, the mood of conscious challenge found its receptive audience. Two of the films in this first programme were made with assistance from the British Film Institute's Experimental Production Fund, which endeavours on the flimsiest of resources to sustain a programme of noncommercial experiment. Two later pictures, *Every Day Except Christmas* and *We Are the Lambeth Boys*, were the result of enlightened sponsorship by the Ford Motor Company, and could afford a professional finish impossible in the first, rougher ventures. Free Cinema set out to celebrate 'the significance of the everyday', to look at jazz clubs and youth clubs and funfairs, at Covent Garden market, at people relaxing and doing their jobs. The impetus was directly social: it was important to Lindsay Anderson that the Covent Garden porters themselves should see *Every Day Except Christmas*, his lyric poem about the place where they spent their days, because 'I want to make people – ordinary people, not just Top People – feel their dignity and their importance.' What are we putting up with in the name of entertainment? asked *O Dreamland*. What do work, when it is mechanical and laborious, and relaxation mean to young Londoners? asked Reisz's *We Are the Lambeth Boys*. The language was didactic and propagandist; and a gulf far wider than the Channel divided the films from documentaries such as Georges Franju's *Hôtel des Invalides* or Resnais's *Toute la Mémoire du Monde* or Agnès Varda's *Du Côté de la Côte*. The French directors were making films which might propagate a point of view; the English felt that the point of view must be propagated.

As recently as 1957, the Free Cinema group asked its audience to view a programme 'In direct relation to a British cinema still obstinately class-bound; still rejecting the stimulus of contemporary life, as well as the responsibility to criticize; still reflecting a metropolitan, Southern English culture which excludes the rich diversity of tradition and personality which is the whole of Britain.' Jimmy Porter's sweet-stall, Arthur Seaton's lathe, and that bare room in *A Taste of Honey* have taken us a long way from this, even though it is significant that none of these images originated in the cinema. Free Cinema marked a necessary stage in the particular journey the British cinema had to take, and its timing was perfect. As a movement it was (and recognized itself to be) in step with that whole semi-cultural, semi-political wave of protest which dates roughly from the time of Suez and Hungary; which asked, in the voice of Jimmy Porter, why 'there aren't any good brave causes left' and found its cause in nuclear disarmament; which voiced a political protest through the *New Left Review* and infiltrated the theatre through the Royal Court and Theatre Workshop. Out of the Midlands and the North and the East End meanwhile came the new regiment of playwrights and novelists, Shelagh Delaney, Arnold Wesker, Alun Owen, Alan Sillitoe, Keith Waterhouse and Willis Hall, David Storey, to overturn that 'metropolitan Southern English' domination. From *Look Back in Anger* in 1956 to the gadfly humours of

'That Was the Week that Was' in 1962, from *The Uses of Literacy* to 'Coronation Street', the lines intersect.

All this has nothing to do directly with the cinema, except in so far as the industry was bound, sooner or later, to accept these influences and make what it could of them. But it took its time, partly because of a natural conservatism and partly because the kind of young talent that in France turned naturally towards the cinema, in England found its way instead into the theatre. After *Look Back in Anger* opportunities existed or could be made to exist for the playwrights, while everyone knew the kind of grinding battle involved in attempting to launch a film career. The cinema had to try to win, on its own account, some of this new freedom of the stage. Significantly, Lindsay Anderson abandoned documentary after *Every Day Except Christmas*, to work in the theatre for five years before coming back to the cinema in 1963 with his first feature, *This Sporting Life*.

Documentary, the theatre – and television. In effect, television shook up a few accepted ideas about what audiences wanted and how they wanted it, just as 'Z Cars' has put a bit of a dent into the image of 'Dixon of Dock Green', which was also that of the cinema's favourite policeman. Television drama discovered that a Harold Pinter play could turn up high in the Tam ratings; TV documentary, on such programmes as 'Monitor', could give directors a scope for individuality increasingly hard to come by in the sponsor-dominated world of documentary cinema. Simply by getting about, moving easily up and down Britain, and poking its cameras into some unconsidered corners, television loosened things up all round.

In the cinema, it was clearly a matter of who would give the first real push. And, with characteristic irony, it was provided by a director who had nothing to do with any of these various outside pressures, but who had grown up in the cinema ever since he ran away from school to join the industry before the war. Jack Clayton had been production manager and producer, had worked with John Huston and Anthony Asquith, had directed a single short-story film, *The Bespoke Overcoat*. When he made his first feature, *Room at the Top*, he was, from his own point of view, simply filming a story he found compelling. Yet, because of the film's sensational earnings at the box-office and because of the ground it covered, the industry is still living in the shadow of this picture.

The public response to *Room at the Top*, both in Britain and America, was immediate and overwhelming. A performance of great integrity by Simone Signoret; a new director who was not afraid, like so many people in the British cinema, to use his camera, to see a film *as* a film, clearly accounted for a lot. But *Room at the Top* already contained any number of the incidents and reference points which have since built up into the new conventions. It talked about sex and class and money; it presented a hero who was almost the classic young man from the provinces, the Julien Sorel of an English north-country town; it moved around in an immediately recognizable industrial landscape; its dialogue had the hard-shelled brusqueness and the occasional piercing moment of self-revelation. And it included the near-ritual beating-up (see also *Saturday Night and Sunday Morning*), the melancholy seaside idyll in the rain (see, if rather less directly, *A Kind of Loving* and *The Loneliness of the Long Distance Runner*), the pub scenes (see the new British cinema, *passim*).

Having signposted the territory, Jack Clayton insisted that he had made a film, not pioneered a movement, kept us waiting almost three years for his next picture, and then directed *The Innocents*. You could scarcely find two novelists with less common ground than John Braine and Henry James, on whose *The Turn of the Screw* Clayton's second feature was based. And this intelligent, visually elegant adaptation of the most quietly chilling of ghost stories confirmed its director's position as a film-maker with a highly developed sensibility and strong aspirations as a stylist. Clayton is one of the perfectionists: an interpretative director, rather than one of those who creates from the ground up, but also a film-maker who would rather take his own line than get caught up on any of the treadmills. His firm refusal to repeat *Room at the Top*, and his decision to film a subject which set him problems involving the finer shades of perception, at a time when the whole trend was towards rougher and more immediate issues, are indications of a personality which has yet to declare itself wholly on the screen, to find a subject on which he will put the unmistakable director's signature.

The Innocents stands apart: main-stream British cinema during the late fifties and early sixties has meant *Look Back in Anger* and *A Taste of Honey* and *The Loneliness of the Long Distance Runner* (Tony Richardson); *Saturday Night and Sunday Morning* (Karel Reisz); *A Kind of Loving* (John Schlesinger); and *Whistle Down the Wind* and *The L-Shaped Room* (Bryan Forbes). And it has meant the *Carry On* series, the Boulting Brothers' *I'm All Right Jack*, Frank Launder and Sidney Gilliat's *Only Two Can Play*, the comedies of disenchantment.

Easy enough to see what these films have in common. Their centre is the provinces rather than London; their idiom is hard (Arthur Seaton does his job, draws his wages, enjoys his Saturday nights, and everything else is 'propaganda'); they get across to their audiences by stimulating identification and a direct response. They are anti-authoritarian, but they are not noticeably celebrating that 'sense of community' which Free Cinema advocated. They dislike a great many of their characters – the television-ruled parents of *A Kind of Loving* and *The Loneliness of the Long Distance Runner*, almost anyone in a uniform, even a bus conductor's, the people who fill their semi-detacheds with knick-knacks. They see life as grey, grimy, and desperately restricted, never more so than in its pleasures, which are taken solemnly and almost always end in quarrels (the seaside row in *A Taste of Honey*; the end of the Skegness week-end in *The*

Loneliness of the Long Distance Runner; the evening out in *A Kind of Loving*). To a formidable extent the films express English puritanism, a melancholia of youth. And, inevitably, it is youth itself that the films sympathize with and respond to, in the persons of that extraordinarily talented generation of young British actors who owe nothing to the West End.

A few years ago, if the British cinema had an immediately identifiable image, it would have been a shot of Kenneth More, jaw boldly jutting, on the bridge of a destroyer. At the moment, the national cinema would more readily be summed up in a view of a boy and girl wandering mournfully through the drizzle and mist of industrial Britain, looking for a place to live or a place to make love. A small group of films, however, could not conceivably have worked this transformation if the public had not shown itself ready. As realism, of a kind, becomes the box-office catchword, film-makers who for years have got along placidly with more genteel doings grit their teeth and turn to sterner stuff: if the hero must be sent slinking about the back alleys of Soho, or discovered being sick just out of camera range, or ranting in pastiche Jimmy Porterisms, then in the name of realism, box-office, and the 'X' certificate it will be done. The public taste has been for the pale-blue jokes of the *Carry On* series, the overt cynicism of an *I'm All Right Jack*, the tough colloquialisms of writers such as Bryan Forbes or the ubiquitous team of Keith Waterhouse and Willis Hall. Tolerably hard to fool, this audience is also hard to move, since a built-in defensiveness mocks at sentimentality and any suspicion that it might be being got at. The *Saturday Night* public is also the *Carry On* and the 'Coronation Street' public: its heroine is Ena Sharples.

Two streams have run significantly parallel: a movement at times ferociously critical (as in John Osborne's plays, or some of Alan Sillitoe's writing) of the values and standards of Britain in the sixties; and a public taste, developed at least to some extent through television, for a surface show of realism and a degree of anti-Establishment cynicism or protest. The new writers and film directors, who may well have felt that they were in for a fight, found part of the battlefield abandoned. Quite a bit of what they wanted to show turned out to be exactly what their audiences wanted to see; and a striking relaxation in film censorship, notably since Mr John Trevelyan's tenure as Secretary of the British Board of Film Censors, has opened paths which only a few years ago would have remained firmly barred. But, at the same time, the cinema has built on foundations well and truly laid for it by the novel and the theatre: almost all the films of note originate in plays or novels, and the writers the cinema acquires for itself remain experts in adaptation. Already the theatre has moved on, so that the cinema, having achieved its belated discovery of naturalism, again runs the risk of being left behind, marooned with its 'X' certificates, its northern skylines, and its tape-recorder dialogue, while the theatre takes another stride forward.

Within a group of films with a great deal of common ground, however, there remain the personal variations in attitude and approach, the deployment of talent. At the centre stands Tony Richardson, by far the busiest of the young directors (five films in about four years), and also the one who has done most to put the whole thing on the map commercially, not only through his own films but through his and John Osborne's company, Woodfall. At first cold-shouldered by the industry, which did not relish being roundly told off for its traditionalism by two young men from the theatre, Woodfall won acceptance with the earnings of *Saturday Night and Sunday Morning* and *A Taste of Honey*. Tony Richardson's energy and determination to bring what was in effect the mood of the Royal Court into British cinema had gained a notable victory.

The tribute 'good with actors' is paid to any number of directors, not always with much justification: Richardson really is good with actors, and good at casting as well as directing them.

But he also brings, from his Free Cinema association, a determination to get out of doors; and it is precisely here that his films so often seem to go adrift. *A Taste of Honey* and *The Entertainer*, in particular, went in for so much in the way of funfairs, street parades, concealed-camera shooting in the streets, singing choruses of children, and all the superficial odds and ends of naturalism, that they blurred the impact of two plays not in themselves naturalistic. *The Loneliness of the Long Distance Runner* makes what one assumes can only be conscious gestures in the direction of the *nouvelle vague*, with its bit of speeded-up action, its frozen final shot, its self-consciously 'cinematic' emphases. But the echoes of *Les Quatre Cents Coups* also point the contrasts: where Truffaut's style grew out of his theme, Richardson's looks the result of a deliberate effort of will, so that the bits and pieces remain unassimilated. Already, in this film, the original spirit of rebellion is seen to be turning towards sterile fretfulness, as the script works its way through the stock juvenile-delinquency situations (the loveless home; the brush with the police; the fight with another boy; the sad little love-scenes) before emerging with its thumbs-down verdict on authority. Richardson can do some things so well (the theatrical things, as might be expected from his background) that one wonders the more at the apparent failures of confidence in his own material which lead him into over-statement. He is a director who seems to do a good part of his thinking in capital letters.

By contrast, Karel Reisz's *Saturday Night and Sunday Morning* and John Schlesinger's *A Kind of Loving* chose something plainer. Arthur Seaton in *Saturday Night* is not, like John Osborne's Jimmy Porter or Alan Sillitoe's own Colin Smith or Shelagh Delaney's quicksilver heroine, a fish naturally out of water. He keeps up his running fight with the obligations society tries to lay on him, but this is not a case of war to the knife: in the end, the housing estate waits to claim him, for all the stones he may throw at it. Where a Jimmy Porter, by design, makes audiences feel ill at ease, they cheerfully accept Arthur and understand his rebellious Saturday; and a good part of the strength of Karel Reisz's film, and of Albert Finney's performance, lay in this accurate placing of a character, this give-and-take between the audience and the screen. Arthur exists within a context of pub and factory, back-to-back houses, and Sunday mornings on the river-bank. Less subjective, and to this extent less adventurous, than the Richardson films, *Saturday Night* tried neither to take a strongly personal stand nor to handle more in the way of general comment than could be assimilated into its immediate, restricted field of vision. Observation ought to precede statement: when Arthur soliloquizes we do not quite believe him, because for the moment he has stepped out of character to remind us not who he is but *what* in social terms he is.

Albert Finney commented, somewhat gloomily, that he could have gone on playing Arthur Seaton for the next ten years. Clearly he could, or at least until the style in heroes changes: the part and the actor were ideally matched, and the truculence belongs as unmistakably to Britain in the sixties as James Dean's wary and nervous rebellion belonged to the America of a few years earlier. The public response here was fundamentally to a character and an actor, whereas in the case of *A Kind of Loving*, a film very similar in its attitudes, one suspects that it was rather to a situation. John Schlesinger's picture, about the working-class boy in a white-collar job, harried into marriage with a girl who feels herself socially a cut above him, again shows the rebel tamed, won over not by the girl's harridan of a mother, entrenched behind her television set, but by the solid nonconformist conscience of his own family. Inarticulate ambition; frustrated tenderness; the world of the job, the office party, the evening out at the pictures; and above all the sense of restriction, meanness, and nagging discontentment: these have been the themes of Britain's new radicals.

Naturalism, of course, has not become the road for more than a group of film-makers. Joseph Losey, the émigré American director of *Blind Date* and *The Criminal*, prefers something more high-powered: film-making in which if one is not immediately made aware of the horsepower under the bonnet one is aware of nothing. Other directors of achieved or intermittent promise – Seth Holt, Cliff Owen, and Sidney Furie – work in different areas. But the film-makers who have taken the train north from London, with a script based on a new play or novel in their brief-cases and a location of soot-streaked buildings and hard asphalt playing-grounds awaiting them, have been able to feel that they were on the main line. In turning their cameras on the day out at Blackpool, the honeymoon at Southport, the competitive drinking in the local, they could feel that they were making up for those years when the British feature cinema tried so hard to conceal from itself that the industrial revolution had ever happened.

Writing about British films, it is said, one talks about what is done: writing about French or Italian films, one discusses how it's done. We are compelled, in other words, to put content before form, for the films have set out to investigate a social landscape rather than to make that discovery of a medium which a director such as Truffaut so rapturously communicates. Our film-makers travel as mass observers rather than as artists prepared to turn the landscape upside down if it happens to suit their purposes. If the French risk irresponsibility, the British risk the elimination of surprise: a situation triggers off a reaction, and the audience knows in advance what the reaction must be, because it knows – or by now should know – the kind of social thinking at work. Free Cinema, a necessary influence only six years ago, now looks like a limiting one, since the didacticism which was so much a part of it lingers on. 'An illustrated guide to current fashion, with every attitude and every statement perfectly predictable,' wrote Isabel Quigly with cruel accuracy of *The Loneliness of the Long Distance Runner*. It is not that the landscape itself becomes over-familiar, but that the film-makers have decided in advance exactly what they expect to find there.

In Lindsay Anderson's *This Sporting Life*, a film more concerned with an emotional landscape than a physical one, there seemed a real awareness of the problem. Too often in a British film, when the director turns his camera on some picturesque bit of urban squalor, one can almost visualize the mobile canteen and the studio cars parked just out of camera range. But in this story of the Wakefield rugger player caught up in a desperate and hopeless relationship with his widowed landlady, the director worked from much further inside his subject. A sequence of a rugger match in slow motion, a moment of grim jousting in the mud, becomes an expression of a man's state of mind. And the result was a film which accepted the English tradition, with its emphasis on narrative and ordered story-telling, but at the same time cracked open the naturalistic surface to achieve an emotional freedom of its own.

But artistically, as well as geographically and economically, Britain's cinema belongs somewhere between America and Europe. Film-making in this country is simply too expensive, too tightly organized, to permit the free flight of, say, a *Tirez sur le Pianiste*. Opportunities for short-film production, which the French experience has indicated to be a prerequisite of an experimental feature industry, are desperately limited. Film-makers in Britain who want to find out where their medium can take them are consequently likely to lag behind the theatre and the novel, to jump into the breaches made for them by other people. But the post-*Room at the Top* era has come near to running its course; and the directors who have emerged from it have to find their own way towards a more cinematic cinema, unaided by influences from across the Channel.

9. Thought Control

However partial or distorted the image one gets of a society through its cinema, it is still possible to discern the national face behind the screen. It is difficult to conceive of a neo-realist idealism without the jubilant preface of the liberation of Rome; or to look at Britain's films of the past few years without reference to our redbrick radicalism; or to ignore the effect of the political climate on a French cinema which declares its awareness of strain in the very insistence with which it puts private before public life, and creation for creation's sake before either. A cinema of dissent or disengagement makes comments no less revealing than one which wholeheartedly endorses the standards of its society. But a cinema without dissent, one built on committee decisions and pre-censorship, can only throw back at us the face of a government.

Totalitarianism, George Orwell argued, must destroy literature:

Imagination – even consciousness, so far as possible – would be eliminated from the process of writing. Books would be planned in their broad lines by bureaucrats, and would pass through so many hands that when finished they would be no more an individual product than a Ford car at the end of an assembly line. It goes without saying that anything so produced would be rubbish;

but anything that was *not* rubbish would endanger the safety of the state.

Even in the cinema, where creation by committee is so much more readily arrived at, this has not happened yet. But if no distinctions are to be recognized between art and propaganda (and Lenin's famous dictum that 'the cinema is *for us* the most important of the arts' implicitly denies them), then the calibre of Soviet cinema at any given moment will depend on how far artists can genuinely identify themselves with whatever causes they are called on to promote, and how wide are the areas within which the propagandist impulse can be disregarded. The dynamic of the Soviet cinema of the twenties was the dynamic of the Revolution; the tedium of the post-war years was a direct consequence of Stalinism, when the Russians built films, as they put up statues, to endorse an iron régime of power. For a while, indeed, the image of the Stalinist cinema showed every sign of congealing into that of Stalin himself.

A thesis could usefully be written around the presentation of Stalin on the screen. The biographies of Lenin made shortly before the war saw Stalin as the loyal number-two man, the father figure accepting the lesser role of jolly uncle. Then came the deification, which achieved its apotheosis in the 1949 *The Fall of Berlin*: Stalin in his garden, delivering his homilies from amidst the flower-beds; Stalin in his office, determining the fate of armies with a glance at a map and a wave of the hand; Stalin descending from the air, benign, white-uniformed, the true god from the machine, arriving in Berlin to claim the salutes and the spoils. Then, after his death, came Khrushchev's denunciation, including the sardonic comment that:

It was only through films that he [Stalin] knew the country and agriculture. And these films had greatly embellished the real situation. Many films so pictured collective-farm existence that tables groaned beneath the weight of turkeys and geese. Clearly Stalin believed that it was really like this. . . .

As André Bazin commented, in a postscript to an article on 'The Myth of Stalin', the fantasy had at last come full circle: 'the deception of the myths recoiled on their central figure himself'. Western or Eastern, wrote Bazin tartly, myths work in much the same way. 'From this point of view, the only difference between Stalin and Tarzan is that the films devoted to the latter do not pretend to documentary accuracy.'

The Nazi rally film *Triumph of the Will*, perhaps the screen's greatest single propaganda document, used stage-managed fact: it showed a real Hitler, a man who might be caught out in the betraying gesture. But a fictionalized Stalin, interpreted by actors, need and could do no wrong; and this deliberate use of the cinema, to build during his lifetime a towering image of the infallible leader, remains something unique in its extremism. The films, one presumes, must now be locked securely in the Soviet archives: just as history, in a Communist state, is subject to perpetual revision in an effort to eliminate intractable and unwanted fact, so a totalitarian cinema finds itself compelled to shed bits of its past.

This sterile period of the Soviet cinema concentrated on solemn biographies, irresistibly reminiscent of three-volume Victorian 'tributes' (Pudovkin did one of an aviation pioneer; Dovzhenko one of a naturalist), and made occasional wild flings into anti-Americanism (one remembers a gallant Soviet girl agent foiling plots all over Germany). In retrospect it is starkly overshadowed by the tragedy of Eisenstein's last years. *The Boyars' Plot*, the second part of his *Ivan the Terrible*, was completed about the end of the war and immediately proscribed, locked away unseen in the vaults until ten years after its creator's death. He had 'portrayed the progressive army of the *oprichniki* as a band of degenerates similar to the American Ku Klux Klan, and Ivan the Terrible, a man of strong will and character, as a man of no will and little character', he was told in a directive from the Central Committee of the Party. Eisenstein's own apologia makes pitiful reading:

We artists forgot . . . those great ideas our art is summoned to serve. . . . We forgot that the main thing in art is its ideological content. In the second part of *Ivan the Terrible* we committed a misrepresentation of historical facts which made the film worthless and vicious in an ideological sense. . . .

Soviet cinema was still governed by the image of the 'positive hero', the man sustained by a total sense of purpose. Eisenstein had transgressed doubly, in admitting doubts and in making a formalist film, possibly the supreme formalist film of all time. Backwards and forwards went the arguments about socialist realism, debated in that Russian critical prose which always reads, in translation at least, as though one were chewing one's way through the soggiest of blankets. Eisenstein himself died in 1948, leaving the third part of *Ivan* among the long list of his unfilmed, uncompleted projects. Then, after the curtain lifted with the death of Stalin, this cinema in its mood of glum self-appraisal needed and was permitted its heroes. The rehabilitation of Eisenstein is complete, with his papers devotedly treasured in the Soviet archives, exhibitions of his drawings sent touring Europe, his banned film released to the world.

A Western critic of the Soviet cinema is always liable to put the emphasis in the wrong place. Firstly, he simply has not seen enough. When he complains that all he does seem to see are war films, records of ballet and opera performances, and versions of the classics, he will be told that these ought not to be regarded as truly representative, and, if the Russian is sophisticated enough, it will be hinted that of course the export policy may be a little restrictive. Then there is the critic's tendency to equate the words propaganda and lie, and to assume that since Western artists could not bring themselves to work under such directives and constraints, and the committee system of checks and counter-checks, Russian film-makers must feel equally shackled. We could not, clearly, expect a screen *Dr Zhivago* at any time; but within the system there may be imposed propaganda and propaganda accepted and promoted as an act of faith. Certainly the Russians are indefatigably self-critical.

The public, wanting art with emotional content, having been choked by films stuffed with dry didacticism and picturing the formal aspects of the lives of the heroes of the past, will jump at any work of art which deals with some of the human aspects of the spirit.

So, in 1954, wrote the veteran director Mikhail Romm. In 1961, Ilya Ehrenburg saluted *Ballad of a Soldier* in very much the same terms:

The urge for modesty and self-restraint – so understandable after the period of false monumentality and stilted obligatoriness in works of art – has manifested itself. . . . Here the lofty is depicted through the commonplace, sometimes the trivial.

During these years, the Soviet cinema had been very consciously endeavouring to rediscover its humanity, while at the same time holding fast to the doctrines of socialist realism, the ideal of a 'positive' cinema if not necessarily a positive hero.

The Russian film remains puritanical about sex, sentimental about children, irreproachably Victorian in its morality. Questioned by a couple of French journalists about Russian reactions to Western films, Sergei Youtkevich, most cosmopolitan of Soviet directors, talked about the negative pessimism of *À Bout de Souffle* and explained the impossibility of showing Antonioni's *La Notte* in a Russian cinema.

The audience wouldn't understand his innovations in screen language. . . . They would just laugh at it all. All that luxury, and those bored people, so lonely and so impotent. And their cars! And their comforts!

Saturday Night and Sunday Morning reportedly shocked Mme Furtseva, former Minister of Culture. And although many more Western films are now imported into Russia, their audiences (whose favourite pictures from the West, it used to be said, included *Lady Hamilton* and the George Formby comedies) are still carefully shielded from any infection by Western melancholy. It is a self-defensive morality.

Russian film-makers, who certainly keep up with the products of Western industries, manage to regard them with a detached curiosity. Their own problems are elsewhere. The dynamic of the twenties, the period when artists had looked on the future and saw that it worked, died long before Eisenstein and Pudovkin. The modern Soviet industry is highly organized: large, well-equipped studios in Moscow and Leningrad, independent headquarters for some of the various republics within the Soviet Union (of which the Georgian has to date produced the most enterprising and individual films); and, as part of the whole state set-up, a film archive and a film school probably unrivalled in the world. Most of the great Soviet directors, including Eisenstein, have taught at the film school, which was founded soon after the Revolution at Lenin's instigation and offers training in six separate faculties. Visiting the editorial office of *Sight and Sound*, the woman editor of Russia's equivalent film magazine, *Isskustvo Kino*, was a little surprised to find a staff of three in a single office: at home, she had sixteen people in ten rooms. But an industry which has abolished the cruder commercial pressures, which devotes so much money and time and enthusiasm to preserving the cinema's past as well as preparing for its future, has still to cope with the difficult present, to get that enthusiasm on to the screen.

War themes recur again and again: in Sergei Bondarchuk's *Destiny of a Man*, in Mikhail Kalatozov's *The Cranes Are Flying*, in Grigori Chukrai's *Ballad of a Soldier* and *A Clear Sky*. These are among the most celebrated of the 'thaw' films, presenting characters infinitely more human, more fallible, simply more interesting, than the propaganda-poster heroes of a decade ago who were encouraged to see life in the relentless terms of production targets. But they are still not quite interesting or complex enough. Symptomatically, all the East European cinemas, not only the Russian, have repeatedly gone back to the war for their subjects. It was of course the great shared experience, the wound that scarred a generation: one would not expect the Russians easily to forget Stalingrad. But war also simplifies matters for the artist, allows for clear-cut issues, undivided loyalties, the sense of purpose imposing its own clarity. Against the contamination of the West, the guilt-ridden movies produced by our own insecure morality, the Russians put up a heroic cinema nearly twenty years out of date.

At the same time, the release from the stylistic dogmas of Stalinism, which had suppressed anything and everything that could conceivably be labelled as formalist, opened the door to more virile and energetic techniques. Kalatozov, a Soviet veteran, and his cameraman Urusevsky, filmed *The Cranes Are Flying* and *The Letter That Was Not Sent* with a remorseless bravura emphasis, using all the camera tricks (hand-held camera; elaborate crane shots; helicopter shots) that the Soviet cinema had schooled itself to disregard. *Destiny of a Man* contains a celebrated shot in which the camera rises vertically, dramatically, from a man lying in a wheat-field until he becomes a tiny dot, a human flower in a great sea of wheat. In Chukrai's *A Clear Sky* a scene of a train passing through a station builds up into an extended symbolic montage, a kind of Eisenstein exercise, in which by intercutting flashing glimpses of the faces in the crowd with the racket of the train the director makes it seem that it will forever go on thundering through that station. Yet, except in isolated instances, all this technique looks like an over-emphatic gloss on nothing in particular. A conscious sophistication at one extreme, a determination to prove beyond all question that the tools have been mastered, clashes with a conscious *naïveté* at the other. The camera dashes wildly all over the place: the figures in the landscape remain static.

Where the Soviet cinema retains all its mastery is in the field of literary adaptation; mostly, of course, from the Russian classics, though one remembers with affection Sergei Youtkevich's *Othello*, with its fine freedom of setting, and Grigori Kozintsev's *Don Quixote*. When it comes to a film like Joseph Heifitz's *The Lady with the Little Dog*, the director, another veteran from the Soviet cinema's middle generation, seems wonderfully sure of his ground. The French can make everybody else's period films look a bit like charades; and the Russians can be even better than the French. Heifitz's adaptation from Chekhov, the story of a melancholy love-affair begun on a Black Sea holiday, continued in snatched and hopeless meetings, is quite effortlessly exact in its details – the listless, lackadaisical atmosphere of a seaside promenade, the lovers' encounter at a provincial theatre, the sense of that timeless world with its great stretches of yawning lethargy and its small gestures towards action. A younger film-maker, Sergei Samsonov, achieved similar results on a minor scale in another Chekhov adaptation, *The Grasshopper*. But it was Heifitz's quiet piece of screen literature, with its resonant melancholy and far-ranging sympathies, which appeared to many Western critics, considerably to the surprise of some of the Russians, an achievement leaving their much-touted *Ballad of a Soldier* standing. And it seems part of the whole paradox of this present Soviet cinema that one should feel so strongly this undertow of proud nostalgia in the Chekhov films; and that their makers should allow, and so sympathetically uncover, in his characters the kind of frustrations and regrets they would jeer at in Antonioni's.

'Loneliness is something which exists in the capitalist world, and perhaps deep in human psychology as well,' says Youtkevich, 'but it's something the cinema ought to fight against.' This sort of ideological insulating tape, liberally applied, has done its job, and the Soviet cinema lays down standards of militancy which the other Communist industries are for the most part prepared to follow, if with only intermittent echoes of

the Russian expertise. Chinese cinema remains virtually an unknown territory, but the few films that have filtered through to
the West are inclined to enjoy plainly bracing titles (*Woman
Basket Ball Player Number Five* lodges itself immovably in the
memory) and to deliver propaganda homilies which Moscow
would regard as elementary. The East Germans have made a
series of scorching documentaries about the ex-Nazis still
allegedly holding down positions of power in West Germany;
and their feature industry, although leaning towards the propaganda tract at its most dogmatic, at least has rather more life
than its inert West German counterpart. (This failure of the
German industry, incidentally, to recover even a shadow of the
old glories of U.F.A. remains one of the odder, and perhaps
sociologically more revealing, aspects of the post-war film.)
Yugoslavia has a wildly inventive and spirited cartoon division,
developed only in the last few years and already outstripping the
feature industry in ideas; Czechoslovakia has Jiri Trnka, the
puppet-film maker *par excellence*, and a subdued, workmanlike
tradition in feature films. Cartoons, puppet films, fantasies such
as the Czech Karel Zeman's *Baron Munchausen* and *An Invention of Destruction*, provide escape routes for the free-ranging
imagination. The slightly stolid, persistently moralizing feature
industries run through the same recurring themes of war, concentration camp, repatriated prisoners, the contemporary slice-
of-life drama centred on a block of flats or a bus-load of people,
and run few imaginative risks.

Yet there are the exceptions. Just about the time of the
Hungarian revolt in 1956 – and hardly coincidentally – there was
a sudden flare-up of excitement in this national cinema, a sense
of an industry at a creative flash-point. Films such as Zoltan
Fabri's *Merry-Go-Round* and *Professor Hannibal*, Imre Feher's
A Sunday Romance, Laszlo Ranody's *Discord*, pointed to an
industry looking for its own way, no longer satisfied blindly to
follow Soviet or any other direction-posts. 'The best moments,'

wrote a young Hungarian émigré critic, Robert Vas, 'are those of pure, unashamed lyricism. . . . Hungary's cinema is not reflective.' And in these films there was the feeling of a rural, local cinema with, as in Feher's bitter-sweet romance of a Sunday soldier, a top-dressing of Central European sophistication and irony. Fabri allegedly saw Welles's *Citizen Kane* more than twenty times as preparation for his own *Merry-Go-Round*, which is symptomatic in itself of the East European directors' ideas about whom they wanted to imitate. And then came the clamp-down: the stories of films cut by the censors or kept on the shelf; the retreat into safe, schematic themes; and the equally familiar self-criticism. By 1959 the director of the state film industry was complaining that 'our ventures to produce real dramas about our contemporary life successively end in failure'.

This glum admission echoed similar pronouncements from Soviet officials. It is the contemporary film that causes all the trouble; and a cinema which asserted as firmly and ponderously as the Stalinist one its right to be dull has any amount of leeway to make up. The missing element in all these films – in the Hungarian peasant dramas, the Czechs' studies in muted urban melancholy, the Russian explorations of their own new frontiers – is, simply, any real suggestion of intellectual force. A facile and demonstrative humanism, utilizing every evocative association of the lyric landscape, the Russian poetry of the soil, every sentimental comment on childhood, young love, gnarled peasant wisdom, makes its emotional assertions. Russian cinema can be easily likeable because it deals in what are called universals. To particularize would be to come up against the bite of ideas, to admit a right of dissent. This cannot be allowed; and any idea that the thaw might mean a deflection of the propagandist purpose was demolished by Khrushchev's celebrated speech of March 1963, which so peremptorily recalled Soviet artists to their official duties.

It has been left to the Russians' Western neighbours to prove that in a modern Communist cinema the ideology need not be allowed irrevocably to destroy the idea. The Poles came relatively late to film-making, with not much of a cinema to speak of before the war. They created the liveliest of all the European film schools; they had their veteran director, in Aleksander Ford; and they trained a new generation – Andrzej Wajda, Andrzej Munk (killed in a car crash during 1961), Jerzy Kawalerowicz, Roman Polanski, Wojciech Has. As with all the East European industries, the war theme has obsessed them, but in this case one has the sense that it has been a genuine obsession, not a retreat, that problems of national identity and purpose are being laboriously sorted out on the screen. In Wajda's trilogy (*A Generation, Kanal, Ashes and Diamonds*) there is a conscious flexing of intellectual muscle. The young workman in *A Generation* discovers the Party, the collective endeavour, the sense of purpose in unity; in *Kanal* the little group of resistance fighters makes its lonely and desperate journey through the sewers of Warsaw; and in *Ashes and Diamonds* we are face to face again with the individual agony – the orders to kill, and the decision in terms not of a bracing official directive but a lonely confrontation of conscience. As in Sartre's *Les Mains sales*, the assassin is a man who can only be right for the wrong reasons, or wrong for the right reasons.

This trilogy can be seen as a closed circle, moving from hope to disillusionment, from conviction back to uncertainty. It makes Wajda's statement about his own generation, and one is very conscious of the young artist nerving himself to put it all down on the screen. Zbigniew Cybulski (Maciek in *Ashes and Diamonds*), with his dark glasses and wind-cheater, is also to stand for the young Pole of the fifties; and the sense of disorientation and uncertainty spreads outwards from the war years towards the present. When Wajda makes a more relaxed and more strictly contemporary film, as in *Innocent Sorcerers*, we are still given a side-long look in the same direction. His young doctor here, with his motor-scooter, electric razor, tape-recorder, and passion for jazz, treats all these proud possessions as trophies: the emptiness and uncertainty begin where the status symbols (in war the machine-gun; in peace the motor-scooter) leave off.

Not surprisingly, Cybulski found himself described as the Polish James Dean (to go along with all the other actors who have worn, with whatever national variations, the face of rebellion). And Wajda's films have themselves come as bulletins from the international front-line, works by a film-maker conscious of the advantages as well as the hazards of his position on the border-line between the two worlds. He can over-strain his talent, move from the telling compression and directness of *A Generation* to the baroque drum-beating and symbolic filigree-work of *Ashes and Diamonds*. The first film came, openly, from the heart; the later one, apprehensively, from the nerves. Wajda has that broad streak of Gothic romanticism which so few Polish artists seem to escape, a taste for the dark and melancholy ritual, as when Maciek and his comrade, alone in a shadowy hotel bar, set light to the vodka glasses and count over the names of the friends who have been killed. He is an artist very specifically conditioned by his age and country, driven by the compulsions which force the Poles to test out their own national identity. There is an air of calculated nerve about their films, like someone stepping out gingerly, but with a derisively confident smile, towards a mine-field. Intellectuals and romantics, they accept for their own cinema the risks dodged by the Russians.

That this romantic temper has its dangers was one of the contentions of Andrzej Muñk, a film-maker less flamboyant than Wajda but equally valuable to the development of the Polish cinema. Munk made a quiet, sober, and impressive picture in *The Man on the Tracks*, a story about an ageing railway worker. Then, in *Eroica*, a two-part film and yet another on a war theme, he took a glancing look at the Polish cult of heroism, the devotion to lost causes precisely because they are lost, the fatalistic acceptance of betrayal. The second part of this spare, controlled film concerns an officers' prisoner-of-war camp living on the legend of the one man who escaped, and unaware that the hero, the symbol on which they depend, is still within the walls, kept in hiding in a boiler-room so that the legend can remain un-diminished. When the man finally dies, Poles and Germans, in a joint face-saving gesture, unite to smuggle his body out of the camp. What is real heroism, asked Munk, the legend or the fact, the gesture or the endurance?

Whether the myths are confronted, as by Munk, or accepted, as by Wajda, they have governed the Polish cinema: the cavalry mounting its last defiant charge against the German tanks; the betrayal of the Warsaw rising; the nation divided against itself, as one resistance faction goes into action against another; and that ultra-symbolic rubbish-dump across which Maciek stag-gers in his death agony.

The war theme has helped to keep everyone's cinema going. For the victors, an adventure story; for the defeated or the occupied, the expiation or the agony or the self-condemnation. In the West, however, the flood dropped away to a comparative trickle from the moment when all the service comedies began to cut the ground from under the feet of the heroics. But the Polish cinema has looked back of necessity, stripping the bandages from a whole series of national scars. When its directors turn in another direction, they may find it easier to move further into the past (Aleksander Ford with *The Knights of the Teutonic Order*, Jerzy Kawalerowicz with *Mother Joan of the Angels*, a version of the Loudun story) than towards the shadowy present.

This is what gives films like Wajda's *Innocent Sorcerers* or Polanski's *Knife in the Water*, which shifts the traditional Polish game of honour to a sexual ground, their exemplary value. They make contact, spark across the East–West frontier. They have absolutely nothing to do with the positive or the progressive;

their standards are their own, their approach to life cool, sardonic, and apprehensive. They admit unease as a basic condition of existence, so that (in Polanski's film especially) to reach out a hand is to subject oneself to a risk of electric shock. The Russians, who congratulate themselves so fervently on their own inability to produce a *Dolce Vita*, have equated uncertainty with pessimism and pessimism with decadence. The trouble, it seems, is that four-square virtues can only be maintained in a state of isolation; and isolation, with the present internationalism of the cinema, looks more forced than splendid.

10. The Major Industries

Internationalism is inescapable, and throughout the last decade or so film critics have been discovering new cinemas. A movie from some previously unknown territory turns up at a European festival, makes its impact, and at once everyone finds out, with some surprise, that the country concerned has been quietly making films for years. Of course many of the industries really are fairly new; and there are not now very many areas left in the world where film-making of some sort is not going on, where film magazines are not busy getting out the articles about Antonioni and Truffaut and Ingmar Bergman. But it must have been a little disconcerting for the Japanese and the Indians, with cinema traditions stretching back to well before the First World War, and outputs which, quantitatively at least, leave modern Hollywood standing, to be taken up popularly in terms suggesting an ill-concealed surprise that they had got so far beyond the stage of the Box Brownie. After all, Japan makes about 400 features a year, and India over 300, whereas Hollywood production has fallen well below the 200 mark.

Japanese films were known in Europe, if in a limited, film-societyish way, long before the war. At least one famous silent picture, *Crossways*, got as far as the National Film Archive in

London. But the post-war discovery (the word, in this context, is inescapable) dates from the Venice Festival of 1951, when Akira Kurosawa's *Rashomon* took the Grand Prix. The story of how *Rashomon* went to Venice has been told in two different versions. According to the simpler, and if only for that reason more probable, the Japanese were anxious to enter a picture, were uncertain about whether they had anything fitting for export, and allowed the advice of an Italian film company's Tokyo representative to overrule their own doubts. (Such misgivings, incidentally, form a recurring theme among Japanese film experts, who are liable to tell Western critics that they cannot possibly like such-and-such a picture because it is 'much too Japanese'.) The other version of the story, for those who prefer to believe in Oriental ingenuity, is that the Japanese producers, anxious to see their industry making its mark internationally, set out to construct a picture with the express object of captivating the West – exotic, but not too dauntingly so, a bit of a mystery, a film made to specifications as a festival sensation.

Whether by accident or design, they pulled it off: *Rashomon* was the Venice sensation, and in 1954 at Cannes Kinugasa's *Gate of Hell* won another top festival award, largely for its ravishing deployment of colour. The value of film festivals, parenthetically, lies precisely in this sudden focusing of attention: while the starlets are pushing each other into the Grand Canal, with the cameramen in anxious attendance, things are happening elsewhere; and the film which would otherwise have to earn its international reputation slowly, from country to country, finds it made in a night, before a fair selection of the world's film trade and Press.

A handful of festival prizes, though, was only a beginning; and it cannot be said that the Japanese cinema has as yet made any very substantial dent in the Western market. Not, in fact, that it needs to. This industry, as Joseph Anderson and Donald Richie point out in their invaluable source-book *The Japanese*

Film, is one of the relatively few big ones surviving in the world which can still hope to remain solvent without bothering over-much about the export market. While other industries were losing their home audiences, Japan was actually building cine-mas. To quote Anderson and Richie: 'In October 1945 there were only 845 theatres in operation in the entire country; by January 1957 there were over 6,000.' Even then saturation point had not been reached, and new cinemas were still opening at the rate of two a day. With only the more expensive films going be-yond the £100,000 mark, with shooting schedules which seem, by Western standards, ludicrously accelerated, and a distribu-tion system geared to rapid exploitation and immediate returns, Japan's industry has even managed to resist television.

A glance through the catalogue regularly put out by Unijapan, the industry's export organization, is certainly no less disillu-sioning, if anything rather more so, than a flip through similar booklets from European sources. Science-fiction fantasies, with monsters limbering up in the streets of Tokyo, endless stories about pearl-divers, with eternal triangles resolved in underwater battles, the basic samurai adventure, or Japanese Western, the unnervingly accurate imitations of Hollywood pulp fiction at its least endearing, all add up to some of the world's more depress-ing entertainment formulas. And, on top of this, young actors and actresses seem to be groomed to look as unJapanese as possible, to bring off the most lightly Oriental adaptation of the fashionable Italo-American style.

According to *The Japanese Film*, in fact, this is one of the more relentlessly commercialized industries. During the fifties the 'big six' companies got together to divide up the home market, each taking command of its own pre-arranged sector:

Thus, Shochiku aimed for the woman audience, with 'home drama' dominating its production schedule; Toho chose the city people, particularly the white-collar workers, with its 'salary-man' films; and Daei went after the teenage audience with its youth films. ... Tohei concentrated exclusively on juvenile-orientated period drama and modern thrillers for children and rural audiences. Shintoho saw money in pictures that the ultra-conservative would favour, particularly military films and those which recalled the good old days. ...

Hollywood in its days of insolent glory never thought of anything quite like this. But the Japanese like to know where they are in the cinema, to establish a genre such as the 'mother film' which will work its way through a thousand variations on *Stella Dallas*.

European wariness about Japanese cinema, which limits the number of films acquired for distribution and means that few of them go really well even at the most specialized box-office, largely originates in a suspicion that all Japanese films move very slowly and in ways mysterious to the West. There is also a pervasive fear that in surrendering to the attractions of an alien kind of cinema, one may be victim of some stupendous oriental leg-pull, or at least allowing oneself to be blinded by the charms of the merely exotic. These attitudes have turned up repeatedly, though perhaps now less frequently, in popular criticism. The idea that Japanese films are unduly difficult, outside the range of anyone not versed in the tea ceremony or the niceties of judo, has left us with the most haphazard and imperfect knowledge of one of the world's great cinemas. It is a gap that badly needs repairing.

Not that the artists who work in this baffling and contradictory industry have had an easy passage. Commercial the set-up may be, but according to Anderson and Richie it is also 'one of the most conservative, artistically reactionary, inefficient and un-professional in the world'. The Japanese director cannot hope, like the Westerner, to get into the cinema by way of a successful script or a period in the theatre. He must expect to follow the laborious and traditional route of assistant, or apprentice, usually advancing to his full professional status only in middle age.

like *The Hidden Fortress* or *Yojimbo*; he has looked into corruption in Japan's big-business society in the strongly melodramatic *The Bad Sleep Well*. This only partly successful film opens, incidentally, with one of the most compelling sequences he has ever shot: a big wedding reception, with press photographers as a cynical chorus, and the sudden wheeling in of a huge cake in the shape of an office building, with a flower dangling from one of the windows to complete this cold memorial to a forgotten crime. Like Bergman or Ford, Kurosawa has his stock company of actors, headed by the drivingly energetic Toshiro Mifune, who move as fluently as the director between the period and the contemporary subject.

In *Ikiru* (known correctly as *Living*, incorrectly as *Doomed*), the story of a tired old bureaucrat, dying and forlorn, who devotes his last months to pushing through a project for a children's playground, we have Kurosawa the socially committed film-maker at full stretch, taking on what might be thought of as a de Sica subject but again demonstrating that Japanese talent for assimilating other people's conventions and making something unique out of them. And in *The Seven Samurai*, in which the seven mercenaries come to the help of a village threatened by bandits, and realize that in the end it is the eternal, ungrateful peasant who survives, one has the Kurosawa of the action picture, assembling the threads of a complex narrative, balancing the character-study against the demands of the duel and the ambush.

Kurosawa remains the only Japanese director with whose work English critics can feel they have much more than a nodding acquaintance. The great Kenji Mizoguchi died in 1956, and of his eighty-eight films only two have been shown commercially in London; nothing by Yasujiro Ozu has breached the commercial barriers, and only isolated films by directors such as Heinosuke Gosho, Tadashi Imai, or Teinosuke Kinugasa have made an appearance. Kon Ichikawa, a younger film-maker with a fine sense of how to control the black-and-white CinemaScope screen, has been better represented. Ichikawa has that unique and sometimes unnerving Japanese ability to hold an equilibrium between explosive ferocity and an almost quietist appreciation of the beautiful. He drives his characters to the ultimate point of physical endurance (as in *Fires on the Plain*, about the Japanese retreat in the Philippines) or mental obsession (as in *Conflagration*, where a young student sets fire to the great golden temple which has been his ideal of beauty); but he preserves his own emotional detachment through a visual technique very consciously aesthetic. *Fires on the Plain* sees its lost soldiers reduced to cannibalism; *Odd Obsessions* is a study in sexual aberration. In the present seller's market for sensationalism, or what can be made to pass as sensationalism, such are the subjects that will find their way on to Western screens.

There remain the invaluable National Film Theatre, the London Film Festival, the European festivals, allowing us at least a tantalizing look at some films from those directors of whom the commercial exhibitors fight shy. What would an average cinema audience, conditioned by Western ideas of screen pace, make of Ozu's *The Tokyo Story*, with its infinitely calm and subtle tempo and motionless camera? This magnificent film, a novelistic exploration of the relations between the generations, of the old couple making their excursion to the city only to find their children too self-absorbed to offer more than the bare gestures of family loyalty, makes only one real demand: that the audience should accept its deliberation, and acquiesce in the discipline which the film-maker imposes on himself by his suppression of the flourishes of personality. Ozu's colour films, such as *Early Autumn*, can be superbly decorative, alive to every detail of a setting. This supreme quietist among film-makers allows us any amount of visual pleasure. But his films remain largely unseen because of the general conviction that anything so slow cannot but be boring, that such tranquillity is not for the cinema.

Ozu is regarded by the Japanese themselves as their supreme traditionalist, a Victorian in an industry with a high percentage of radicals. He resisted the blandishments of the sound film much longer than most film-makers, directing a silent picture as late as 1934, and his area of subject-matter has been deliberately narrowed down to a fine point of concentration. Repeatedly he has come back to this single theme of the family, the tensile strengths and frayed weaknesses of relationships. 'Pictures with obvious plots bore me,' he says. He stations his camera at eye level, and sets his actors down to talk; he focuses the camera on a corridor, a doorway, and people move across its line of vision; he uses the hint, the suggestion, the half-smile, where other film-makers would insist on statement. His films hold that dramatic distance which the cinema, with its constant and anxious nudging for an audience response, so rarely thinks about: the sentimental reaction is stifled, the emotional forces held in a delicate balance.

But Ozu is not, any more than Kurosawa, a 'representative' Japanese director. The pull towards traditionalism, the stories of families holding together against the pressures from outside, is strongly felt. Equally characteristic is the radicalism of film-makers like Masaki Kobayashi, director of the war trilogy *Ningen no Joken*, a militant anti-militarist. That this is a society living under very high pressures could be gathered from the content and manner of its films alone. The urgent response to things American, the legacy of the occupation, and the tribute of the defeated to the victors, vies with the fear that in this response may be contained a betrayal; the reaction against ceremonial accompanies a recognition of the national dependence on order and discipline; Hiroshima itself becomes a city of bus tours and juke-boxes, a neon-blazing cemetery. The Japanese live, with difficulty and awareness, in the midst of all the contradictions history has piled up around them.

This ever-present historical sense is something almost

unique in a national cinema. Western audiences will tend to see all samurai films as set in some vaguely medieval past, and will be slightly surprised when, in *The Seven Samurai*, guns are trailed by the soldiers. And although the Japanese have on the whole preferred to export their period films, presumably on the theory that Western audiences will find the really remote less intimidating than the familiar viewed from an unaccustomed angle, anyone seeing the period films of a Kenji Mizoguchi will be aware of allusions and subtleties which are bound to pass him by, of the director's ability to assume a continuity between past and present not experienced with our own more self-conscious excursions into history.

'It is not likely that anyone in the West will be able to think of the Japanese film and, for years to come, not also think of Kenji Mizoguchi,' declare Anderson and Richie. Again, this is an artist almost unknown to the English filmgoer, although his work has been much more widely seen and admired in France. When *Ugetsu Monogatari* ('monogatari' merely means 'story'), probably Mizoguchi's most famous film, eventually reached London in 1962, most of the critics gave it a cool welcome. Yet in Venice, when five of the director's films were shown at the 1957 festival in a posthumous tribute, the press filed in at nine-thirty in the morning, to grapple with pictures unsubtitled or titled in languages incomprehensible to most of the audience. Did the English press, not for the first time, react against a reputation?

Ugetsu Monogatari is a story of war and greed, of human love and the illusory love of a phantom princess. Its background figures are the warlords, samurais, and mercenaries of the sixteenth century; its plot concerns a village potter, lured away to a ghost castle where a shadow princess pines for the love which eluded her in life. The images of the film – the misty lake, with a boat rearing up like a phantom ship out of the darkness, the potter's wife waving farewell from among the lakeside reeds, the lovers' silken mat spread out on the grass, the gravely beautiful final shot, when the camera moves up and away from the wife's village grave, out to the fields where life and work continue – are those of a poet who thought like a painter. This most conscious of camera artists could hardly bring himself to compose a shot without some element of beauty.

To the Japanese, Mizoguchi was essentially the painter of women: the geishas whom he studied in so many films; the lost lady of *The Lady of Musashino*, wandering forever by a misty lakeside; the woman who faces crucifixion with her lover in *Chikamatsu Monogatari*; the princess of *Ugetsu*, with her bright silks and ghost-pale face. *Ugetsu*'s title has been rendered into English as *Tales of the Pale and Mysterious Moon after the Rain*, evoking the lake-poetry side of an artist who was also, and toughly, a realist. In a career dating back to the silent period, Mizoguchi made an enormous number of films, most of them never shown in the West. But we have seen enough to know that here is one of the handful of great artists who have chosen this twentieth-century medium rather than any other. It is the strength of the Japanese cinema, which obviously commits no fewer follies than other national industries, that it manages to come to terms with genius.

While Japan has been building cinemas, the other great Asian industry has taken to the roads, with mobile projection units bringing films to the villages outside the range of town cinemas. Japan's audience has been to a considerable extent an urban one, India's very much less so; and this may go some way towards explaining why Indian cinema has been so very much harder for the West to take. Until a few years ago, at least, any Indian film seemed interminable, made even rougher going by a style of popular acting which has all the subtlety of a slap in the face, and by the national custom of lacing any and every film with songs, inserted more or less appositely into the action like so many exclamatory punctuation marks.

India's film industry is large and decentralized, serves an audience deeply attached to the star system, and is subject to some ferocious criticism in the Indian film press, which shows a fine disregard for any laws of libel. A film in Bengali will not easily be understood in Bombay, which means that an Indian director is not working for a public of the whole nation. Popular actors dash from one production to another, not uncommonly contriving to act in two or three films at the same time; and directors may find themselves working on a couple of films simultaneously, to fit in with the comings and goings of their stars. Films remain extremely cheap by Western standards, actors (as in Japan) are not very highly paid, and equipment is sometimes in short supply. To shoot a particular sequence in *Jalsaghar*, Satyajit Ray had to borrow lights from every possible source in Calcutta.

Indian cinéastes are likely to complain that they get few opportunities to see the really important European films, though their cinema has long admitted the influence of Hollywood in staging spectacular scenes, with home-grown deMilles turning every set into a minor Taj Mahal. An extravaganza such as *Aan* achieved the ultimate in this determination to leave nothing out that could possibly be crammed in. Towards the middle fifties, however, a group of films such as Bimal Roy's *Two Acres of Land* and K. Abbas's *Munna* showed the neo-realist influence, powerful if belated. Here was a cinema clearly preparing to break with some of its more laborious conventions.

Then, at the Cannes Festival of 1956, the revelation: Satyajit Ray's *Pather Panchali*. Ray was a young commercial artist from Calcutta, a member of a family which occupies among the intellectual aristocracy of Bengal rather the position of, say, the Huxleys in Britain. In 1950, when Jean Renoir was in Calcutta to make *The River*, Ray had watched him at work, been told by him that 'you would be making great films here if you could only shake Hollywood out of your system', and had written of Renoir (for *Sequence*):

There is nothing more important in a film than the emotional integrity of the relationships it depicts. Technique is useful and necessary in so far as it contributes towards that integrity. Beyond that it is generally intrusive and exhibitionist.

Several years after writing what now has all the air of a credo in the form of a comment, he set out to make his first film, with, he has recorded, 'a unit of eight of whom only one had previous professional experience' and 'an old, much-used Wall camera which happened to be the only one available for hire on that particular day'. The film begun in these daunting conditions of near-amateurism took over two years to complete, before it was finally finished with backing from the Government of West Bengal.

It is difficult [wrote Ray] to describe the peculiar torments of a production held up for lack of funds. The long periods of enforced idleness produce nothing but the deepest gloom. The very sight of the scenario is sickening, let alone thoughts of embellishing it with details or brushing up the dialogue. . . .

Only the sentimentalists who like to think that poets do their best work in garrets will assume that these are the circumstances in which masterpieces get made. *Pather Panchali* remains one of the exceptions.

Ray followed this first film with *Aparajito* and *The World of Apu*, to make up a work of sustained poetic continuity comparable in the cinema only with Donskoi's Maxim Gorki trilogy. *Pather Panchali*'s setting is the village, with the children growing up, the father a harried clerk who would rather be a poet, the mother engaged in a perpetual struggle against hunger. The boy Apu and his sister run through a field of flowers to watch the express train thundering through; and in the later films, as the action moves away from the peasant world into the city, this train motif will recur again and again. The student Apu brings his wife to his room by the railway tracks; hears of her death there; comes near to suicide on the line. Railways and rivers give us the sense of scale and movement, so that although the trilogy is essentially an intimate, close-up work it has nothing enclosed about it.

François Truffaut is said to have walked out of *Pather Panchali*, announcing with surprising asperity that he wasn't interested in a movie about Indian peasants. One London critic ingloriously described the film as a case of 'Pad, pad, pad through the paddyfields'. But the suggestion that the film hardly rated sophisticated Western attention died a rapid death: one of the problems critics have encountered in discussing Ray's work, in fact, is that he is so obviously a highly sophisticated artist. Like Renoir, he looks, and looks, and looks again; builds his films through painstaking observation; assists his players (some professional, many not) to act with that suggestion of unaffected naturalism which looks spontaneous and means hours of the most concentrated patience. Ray is no peasant, and the limpid clarity of his style is not achieved by luck or chance. Within a given human context – the ageing nobleman of *Jalsaghar*, brooding over the music he loves more than life, the young clerk in an episode of *Two Daughters*, caught up, like an E. M. Forster hero, in the most ludicrous of formal tea parties, Apu reciting poetry to the night – Ray knows precisely the values he intends to emphasize, the kind of sympathies he wants us to bring to a scene. Ray has talked of a possible film of *A Passage to India*; and the affinities with Forster, including the humour, and the gentle stubbornness, are obvious enough.

Ray came along to recharge the batteries of humanist cinema at a time when neo-realism had sacrificed its momentum. But if *Pather Panchali* was direct statement, his later films have been a good deal more complex. In *Jalsaghar* the protagonist is an exquisitely selfish old aristocrat, redeemed by the fact that his devotion is to an ideal of beauty. His crumbling estate, with a solitary elephant padding about the grounds, is held as a stronghold against the new men, whose lorries roll by along the road. Ray's heroes are the failed poets, the unpublished writers, the perpetual students, men living with dreams in a world in which authority (as in *Kanchenjunga*) makes jokes, in English, about cricket and talks seriously about money. Again the parallel is obvious: the rumble of the lorries comes like the axe put to the cherry orchard. But Ray's links are also with the Indian village, with his native Bengal; and as a school of young directors grows up around him in Calcutta, so this city begins to look to the outside world like the centre of Indian cinema. Until someone else comes along to change it, Satyajit Ray's Bengal will be the cinema's India.

11. The Movie-Makers

Among all the paradoxes and contradictions of the modern cinema, one of the most obvious and inevitable is the division between a proliferating internationalism and the emergence of all the new and self-conscious national industries. At exhibition level, the great influence for internationalism remains the film festival, with new ones still sprouting at a rate which suggests that a festival has become the next stage in urban development after street lighting and the public library. The festivals act as genuine clearing-houses; and as the number of festivals continues to catch up all too rapidly on the number of films, so the chance of any work of real quality being overlooked recedes. Writers about the cinema have opportunities to know what is going on, at first hand, which are denied to professionals in those arts more dependent on translation.

But internationalism is also a matter of production: film companies set up for a single picture sail under their own flags of convenience, with registered offices in Lichtenstein or Morocco; co-production brings off a series of unnatural alliances between half the countries of Europe; some American directors clearly choose to work almost anywhere that is not Hollywood, partly no doubt because in doing so they can maintain a discreet distance between themselves and their employers, enjoying a freer hand than the front office customarily allows them. At the same time, obstinately, national cinemas continue to look exactly like what they are: Britain, France, Italy go their entirely separate ways, in spite of all the obvious forces at work to pull them closer together. Take the sound-track off a movie, and no audience with any pretensions to experience should have too much diffi-culty in guessing where it comes from. And as the number of film-producing countries increases, so do all those variations in national styles and attitudes which seem, in the long run, even more revealing than the areas of common ground. When the new African states begin to produce their own films, instead of employing other people to do it for them, what may they be able to make of the cinema? What will *we* make of what *they* make? And, conversely, the films made by artists with an intensely sophisticated attitude to movies, such as the tight little *Cahiers du Cinéma* group of directors, must signify less and less as they get further away from their starting-point. If *La Notte* means nothing to Moscow, what does *Vivre sa Vie* mean to Ghana, or *Jules et Jim* to Chile? Hollywood built on its great inter-national stars, the Chaplins and Garbos, and on the entertain-ment conventions it laid down for the world. Now that so many of these conventions are being abandoned, under pressure of the changing times, the film as a film is increasingly left to make its own way in the world.

So far, I have concentrated on national industries, because out of some specific set of economic and social conditions, out of the kind of audience being served and the kind of creative pres-sures at work, the variations in cinema inevitably evolve. But there remain also the film-makers who have fitted into no set pattern, the mavericks and individualists who carry their own creative baggage around with them, or the men who have so dominated their national cinemas (like Satyajit Ray) that we see a country through the films of a single director. Ten years ago,

Indian cinema was an unknown territory; five years hence, one can wager with some confidence, the Latin American countries will have staked a sizeable claim to world attention. And after that . . . Egypt, or Turkey, or the Philippines, or anywhere else which suddenly turns up with a film or two to catch a festival audience's imagination. But of course the patterns also repeat themselves; and within the limited space of this survey perhaps the picture may best be blocked in by looking at the individual record, the pressures confronted and withstood by half a dozen artists with nothing in common beyond a determination to make movies in their own way: Luis Buñuel, film-maker in Mexico, in Spain, in France, and an artist, if ever there was one, who imposes his own mental landscape on whatever part of the world he happens to fetch up in; Leopoldo Torre Nilsson, doyen of the directors now emerging in Latin America; Juan-Antonio Bardem and Luis Berlanga, and their younger colleagues who are trying to haul the censor-ridden Spanish cinema forward into this decade; Ingmar Bergman, who has so dominated Swedish cinema that he has remade people's ideas of it in his own image; Michael Cacoyannis, by no means a Bergman but still a name synonymous with his country's cinema; and Orson Welles, more peripatetic even than Buñuel, the talent no industry has found itself big enough to hold.

A Buñuel film is like raw spirit poured straight on to an open wound, a stinging, cauterizing therapy of shock.

I am against conventional morals, traditional phantasms, senti-mentalism, and all that moral uncleanliness that sentimentalism introduces into society. Bourgeois morality is for me immoral, and to be fought. . . .

He has been fighting it, weapons, strategy, and tactics almost un-changed over the years, ever since *L'Âge d'or*, that surrealist testament, was first shown in Paris thirty-three years ago and the police had to be called in to clear the cinema. When Buñuel made

. *Viridiana*, in 1961, the censors were once more put on their mettle. (*L'Âge d'or* is still probably too explosive for public screening, even if it were permitted outside the safe confines of the National Film Theatre.) A recognition of how far *Viridiana* reaches beyond blasphemy also gave evidence of how fast and thoroughly ideas of what is or is not fit for public performance have been changing. And the press, from *The Times* ('perhaps one of the last masterpieces in the chequered history of surrealist art') to the journals of the Left, to those Catholic critics who could not but respect and detest, were for once united almost across the board.

At the end of the war Buñuel was little more than a name in the cinema text-books, a film-maker who had not been heard from in more than a decade, a survivor from the remote enthusiasms of surrealism, an exile from his own country who had vanished into obscure film jobs in Hollywood and New York. Then, in 1950, came *Los Olvidados*, not the first of his Mexican films but the one which unmistakably signalled his return as an artist who had surrendered none of his old ability to disturb. Set in the shanty-town slums of Mexico City, the study of an urchin gang brutal-ized beyond hope of recovery, subjects for comprehension rather than regret, *Los Olvidados* retains the authentic quality of nightmare, the old surrealist shock transported this time to a realistic setting. Buñuel refuses to compromise the desperation and violence of his theme: the anarchist sees the world as a place of horror, and he is not going to suggest that a little goodwill and a few social workers could put it to rights. There followed *El*, a blinding study in paranoia, the impish black comedy of *Archibaldo de la Cruz*, and in 1953 his entirely unexpected version of *Robinson Crusoe*, an account of the desolation of the one man alone, but also of the small human triumphs – the meeting with Man Friday, the coming to terms with nature – done with an affection and even a serenity to confound critics of Buñuel the black sadist.

Filming in Mexico, in an industry where pictures tend to be very slow and tourist-beautiful to watch, or else highflown exercises in whip-slashing melodrama, Buñuel has had to work quickly and roughly, turning out routine chores, making even his major films in three or four hurried weeks. He went back to France to film; returned to Mexico to direct *Nazarin*, an exposition of the impossibility of an attempt to live as a modern Christ. Then, incautiously given an official invitation to return to Spain, he took the same theme a step further in *Viridiana*, in which the young novice from the nunnery, with her beggars' settlement and her faith in good works, unleashes only that hypocrisy and violence which for Buñuel go hand in hand with the professions of piety. *Viridiana* caused an uproar, with the Spanish government invoking international agreements in a hurried bid to keep the film off foreign screens, as it had most effectively kept it off its own. But Buñuel himself had gone back to Mexico, to complete one of the swiftest and most unswerving right-and-lefts in film history with *The Exterminating Angel*. Here, with inexorable comic logic, he takes a group of people to an evening party and keeps them there, trapped with their own fantasies. In this bland nightmare a bear loiters on a staircase, a disembodied hand clutches at a throat, sheep trot blithely to church. The putrefaction, however, is real.

In the true surrealist tradition, Buñuel makes public his own obsessions, sexual and religious. He cuts through the cinema as cleanly as a flame-thrower, filming in the unerring, unmistakable strokes of a Picasso, delivering himself of the plainest statements, putting neither more nor less than he needs to on the screen. The most telling episode in *Viridiana* is not the beggars' orgy, that blasphemous Last Supper, but the little scene in which a man frees a dog trotting behind a peasant's cart, and another dog promptly replaces the first victim. So much for charity...

Perhaps, like Lawrence, Buñuel is only an inverted idealist. Perhaps it is his great tenderness, the great purity and poetry of his vision, which forces him to reveal the abominable, the malicious, the ugly and the hypocritical falsities of man. . . . Either you are crazy, like the rest of civilized humanity, or you are sane and healthy like Buñuel. And if you are sane and healthy you are an anarchist and throw bombs.

So Henry Miller wrote in the thirties, in a salute from one rebel to another. Perhaps the most extraordinary thing about Buñuel is that, while thirty years have given his work critical respectability, the terms used in writing about it are entirely unchanged.

Buñuel is one of the inimitables, his vision remaining his own, his spare techniques offering nothing to the copyist. But, inevitably, his influence has been felt, and there is more than a touch of the master in some of the work of Leopoldo Torre Nilsson, leading director of the Argentinian cinema, himself the son of a film-maker, and an artist who, like so many of the best in the Spanish-speaking world, attacks the muffled hypocrisies of a society living behind closed shutters. Torre Nilsson and his wife and scenarist, Beatriz Guido, have a favourite theme: innocence corrupted, innocence as the dupe of experience, innocence advancing in trepidation and hope upon its own destruction. Fair young girls move stealthily about shadowed rooms; upstairs (in *The Hand in the Trap*) an old woman, a Miss Havisham of Buenos Aires, lives with her ghosts and her terrors; children (in *La Caída*) are capricious, anarchic, forever sitting down to extraordinary meals, while the prudish young girl who looks after them waits for the assault on her own sensibility; behind the shutters again (in *The House of the Angel*) innocence invites tragedy; up against a wall (in *Fin de Fiesta*) a man is being shot, while a boy learns about the power that corrupts.

Appropriate to such themes is a technique in which shots are heavily angled, interiors shadowed and threatening, in which a pale young face will be filmed in sad close-up against the background of a dark garden. Mannered this director certainly is; and one feels, as with so many of his contemporaries, that the

baroque style is worn with a certain defiance, a conscious asser-
tion of personality and intent. The Argentinian film-makers feel
their affinities with Europe, admit the European influence; un-
heralded, scraps of Antonioni or Bergman or Fellini are liable to
turn up in their work. Castro's Cuba, in one of its first post-
revolutionary actions, issued what virtually amounted to an open
invitation to the left-wing talents of Europe to come and work
with its own film-makers. In these expanding cinemas of
Central and South America, the determination to catch up with
Europe goes with a resolve that whatever the national quality
may be, it ought not to be smothered. Torre Nilsson has made a
style, if a limiting one, his own; his younger Argentinian colleagues (Fernando Ayala, maker of *El Jefe*, Rodolfo Kuhn,
director of *The Sad Young Men*) are still looking around for a
convention to work in. And the Gothic elements in Torre Nilsson's films, the suggestions of long corridors with dark discoveries waiting at the end of them, seem a natural enough
refinement in a national cinema where popular taste has been on
the side of the naïvely melodramatic.

Although audiences do not necessarily get the cinemas they
deserve, a public consistently satisfied with the second-rate will
certainly hold down the creative level of this industry, as it so
patently does that of television. The artist starting from scratch
in a new industry may even have a rather easier time of it than
the one combating a whole arid tradition of 'white telephone'
novelettes or cut-price imitations of the worst of Hollywood. In
any case, in the collective enterprise of film-making, some sort
of strong national tradition counts for a great deal. The lone
director, garlanded with his festival prizes, still has to confront
his national industry on its own level. If he has to fight hardened
conventions in camerawork or set design, or acting mannerisms
of blatant theatricality, his job becomes that much the more
taxing.

Movements towards a more vital cinema tend to begin with an

element of social attack: what will be asked for, critically and by the younger directors, is *verismo*, truth to life, a cinema more closely and critically involved in what Torre Nilsson calls 'the little human truths' about the way people live. Far beyond any specific neo-realist influence is a more general and pervasive conviction that cinema should be in the sort of moral relationship with society that the Pilkington Report saw as a necessity for television. Even a crude form of social commentary will be felt to be on the right track: at least, it gets away from the endless repetition of things which any half-competent Hollywood film-maker can do with his eyes shut, and which look inept and silly when copied with so much heavy-breathing effort. Certainly this holds true not only for Latin America but for Spain, where the careers of Juan-Antonio Bardem and Luis Berlanga, the two best-known directors, have been punctuated by reports of films interrupted, projects shelved, even the hazards of arrest. The film-maker becomes, of necessity as well as choice, a social critic as he tries to break into the areas battened down by censorship.

Since Italy became more expensive, Spain has been one of Hollywood's favourite locations. The more barren the countryside, the more easily it can be made to stand in for almost anywhere – the American West, China, Arabia, even on occasion Spain itself. As has already happened in Italy, a national industry of modest traditions finds itself acting as host to the more grandiose fantasies of world cinema – to *King of Kings*, and *The Fall of the Roman Empire*, and *55 Days at Peking*. A programme of co-production, mainly with Italy, meanwhile helps to pull this cinema out of its previous isolation; and, in fact, Spanish film-making often enough looks like Italian film-making minus the national genius. Bardem early established himself as a director to watch, erratic, intelligent, eclectic, though if one compares his *Death of a Cyclist* with Antonioni's somewhat similar *Cronaca di un Amore*, there is no question of who stands better in the comparison. And, again, there is the temptation to snatch a toe-hold in the international market. Bardem's *Calle Mayor*, a genuinely touching account of life behind the provincial shutters and of a girl cheated out of marriage, suffered from the illusion that an American actress (Betsy Blair, from *Marty*) could be fitted into this Iberian townscape. Bardem lately seems to have been giving his inclination to melodrama an increasingly long rein, while Luis Berlanga, with perhaps more creative stamina, remains the director of genial fables – a *Welcome Mr Marshall*, a *Calabuch*, about an American physicist who would rather make fireworks in Spain than bombs in the United States, a *Placido*, in which the hypocrisies of the charitable are given an uninhibited working over. A rather blacker comedy, Marco Ferreri's *Il Cochecito*, which describes the obsessive campaign conducted by an old man who wants a wheelchair to ride about in, pursues the same method of masked social comment. Unless the *Viridiana* incident proves to have jolted it too severely, Spanish censorship is loosening up; and a group of radical young film-makers and critics stands poised to move in on any ground ceded to them.

But censorship is only one problem: some of the others the career of a director such as Michael Cacoyannis throws into relief. Cacoyannis, a Greek who had lived in England and worked here as an actor, first made his name as the director of the engaging *Windfall in Athens*, a comedy of a disputed lottery ticket, which might have seemed a little derivative from a French film-maker but which here had all the lures of a new landscape, a new actress, in Ellie Lambetti, a new tone of voice. *Stella* and *A Matter of Dignity* took Cacoyannis several stages further: here was a film-maker working with very limited resources, getting about and around his own country, making the kind of picture whose rough, eager vitality earned salutes at that time when Hollywood had gone over to its melancholy worship of production values and energy was at a premium. But the film-maker will try to enlarge his own range, to escape from both the over-restricted budgets and the feelings of provincialism. Cacoyannis tried it with *Our Last Spring* and *The Wastrel*, both filmed in English. The second film was one of those disasters every director seems to experience once in his career; the first a case of misdirection, of good ideas on paper never quite realized on the screen. One was made intensely aware of how difficult it is today to jump the gap between the small national industry and world-class film-making – whatever that illusory dream of directors may be. Once the film-maker simply went to Hollywood: now Hollywood, in the form of its stars, its contracts, its publicists, is more likely to come chasing after him, as the travelling circuses move around the world. Caught in an exposed position, out on his own, an artist needs more than talent to survive.

One who indisputably has this is Ingmar Bergman, that rock on which so many critical toes have been stubbed. Bergman chooses to work with his own accustomed unit around him, spending the winter in the theatre, the summer in the cinema. And he has the immeasurable advantage that behind him piles up a whole unshakeable tradition of film-making, linking his own work to that of Sjöström, Sweden's major director from the silent cinema, and Sjöberg, who still makes occasional films but who has never quite repeated the success of the 1951 *Miss Julie*. When Sjöberg made *Frenzy*, in 1944, the young Bergman worked on the script; when Bergman made *Wild Strawberries*, in 1957, the octogenarian Sjöström played the principal part.

Now in his mid forties, Bergman has behind him a volume of work which few people of his generation in the cinema can begin to equal. In a country with only a limited output of films at the best of times, and where strike action has more than once brought the industry almost to a dead stop, he has directed or collaborated on more than twenty-five films. He has written many of his own scripts; he has assembled that dazzling company of players – Max von Sydow, Gunnar Björnstrand, Eva

Dahlbeck, Harriet Andersson – whose performances he orchestrates through film after film. More has been written about him, in wilder and more extreme terms, than about any other post-war film-maker: his symbolism has been detailed and catalogued; his childhood, in a strict Swedish parsonage, examined; his work has been analysed in terms of Sweden's notorious 'neutrality complex'; he has been called a masochist, a misogynist, a puritan, and, in a cruelly enlightening phrase, 'the best German director of the post-war cinema'. Five years or so ago, when it was impossible to pick up a magazine without finding the obligatory Bergman article, phrases like 'the Shakespeare of the cinema' were tossed freely around.

To attract all this, a film-maker needs to have something oracular in his make-up, in the sense that one consults the oracle not for a clear message, but for the satisfaction of deciphering the riddle. Although Bergman's symbolism is far from impenetrable, his attitude to his characters, stretched so agonizingly on the rack of his imagination, invites speculation. Those middle-aged married couples, quarrelling so bitterly in cars and trains; the old professor in *Wild Strawberries*, his life a blank filled in by the symbols of academic achievement, taking a pilgrimage through his past; the charlatan in *The Face*, a magician in spite of himself; the father in *The Virgin Spring*, conducting a ritual purification before embarking on the slaughter of the men who have raped and killed his daughter; the Knight at his chess game with Death in *The Seventh Seal*: they all dance to the strings pulled by their creator, expressions of his ironic despair at the russian roulette of existence, his questioning of the nature of belief. Bergman can appear almost sadistically brutal to these people of his invention; and then, suddenly, he lets up, flooding the screen with images of innocence and delight. Pain and pleasure alternate: the revolver hammer clicks again on an empty chamber, and the relief is exquisite. These flashes of happiness and tranquillity – the picnic in *The Seventh Seal*, the shots of lovers by lakesides, of sunlight and water, the rapturous surge of ironic glee at the end of *The Face* – are outdoor moments, summer moments held against the long Swedish night.

Bergman has worked through a Germanic brand of expressionism, straight realism (notably in early films such as *Hamnstad*), the historical morality of *The Seventh Seal*; he has juggled with dreams and reality, past and present, truth and illusion, the line that separates the artist as a performer from the artist as a man; he has told us that it is both necessary and miserable to love; he has taken us on a tour of the Swedish soul, so that no article purporting to explain that enigmatic country is now complete without its set of Bergman references; he has worked around the themes of destiny and free will. To his brilliance as a *metteur en scène*, a manipulator of effect, the crystalline tragicomedy of *Smiles of a Summer Night* offers sufficient witness. He has made films which everyone admires, and films which only the extreme Bergman enthusiasts want to see again: he has done so much that commentators on his work can pick up half a dozen separate threads as guides through the Bergman maze. Yet the mists thicken round the oracle, whose northern cave provides such a bleak frontage on life. If one finds his world antipathetic, it may be because, as in a Graham Greene novel, one feels that in shutting off the doors of escape to his characters the artist is taking over the role of destiny. Bergman robs a mother of her child, sends a witch to the burning, puts the revolver with its single bullet to the temple of a man weary of life. Is it fate, or Bergman, who decides who dies and who lives? It is this sense of the ring-master, touching up an act with a flick of his whip, that sets up a resistance.

Bergman's career is almost unthinkable, in practical terms, outside the specific circumstances which have nourished it: a small industry, but one with a formidable tradition and a high conceit. Now that he has become a highly marketable commodity, he could work anywhere; and the Swedish industry can export, not always to his advantage, the apprentice works of its major artist. But Bergman was first able, in an unusually enlightened set-up, to work his way through his own experiments. In this intensely high-pressure business, where it is truer than ever, in a commercial sense, that a director is as good as his last picture, this opportunity for an artist to develop in his own time, through his own errors and discoveries, goes to the very few.

This running fight between the artist and his backers, his demands and their financial safeguards, has engaged many of the big creative talents at one time or another. And Hollywood, above all industries, has been haunted by the grim battles of its past: the memory, for instance, of what it almost let von Stroheim get away with in the twenties, the thousands of feet of film never seen on the screen, the movies cut to ribbons to knock them into some kind of commercial shape. Hollywood beat von Stroheim, just as, twenty years later, it fought Orson Welles to a standstill. Having worked in the cinema for much the same number of years as Bergman, Welles has made infinitely fewer films; and these, for the most part, have been cut about by their proprietors. We have never seen even *The Magnificent Ambersons* in the form its creator originally intended. Welles has had to work either very slowly, as on *Othello*, on which the money was constantly running out and the company dispersed and brought together again, or else very fast. His *Macbeth* was shot in an incredible three weeks for Republic, a horse-opera company taking an unaccustomed flier into culture; and it looked, perhaps not surprisingly, as though it had been knocked off between shifts at the coal face.

Welles came to Hollywood with his own company from the Mercury Theatre, cast them in *Citizen Kane* and *The Magnificent Ambersons*, saw the company disbanded and players like Agnes Moorehead and Joseph Cotten going on to independent stardom. He was twenty-six when he made *Citizen Kane* in 1941; and one of the things that strikes you at any re-seeing is how magnificently, confidently, irresistibly young a film it is. Watching it for the first time, as so many of my generation must have done, during some wartime school holiday, one got a first conviction that if the cinema could really do *that*, it could do almost anything. The spectator is still caught up in Welles's sense of infinite possibility. *Kane* is a movie made in pursuit of a dream – a Gatsby among motion pictures.

Welles, the film-maker who listed prestidigitating among his recreations in *Who's Who*, has never ceased to be a conjuror, a manipulator, a hypnotist. From the best of his fifties films (the thriller *Touch of Evil*, or the untidy rough sketch of his *Othello*) to the worst (*Confidential Report*, which offers so much more show than sense), that power remains unchanging. The voice addressing us from the screen is as instantly recognizable as his speaking voice; and only Welles, in delivering the narrative to *King of Kings*, would have taken it upon himself to give such unfamiliar value to the 't' in apostles. The deep focus, developed with the cameramen of *Kane* (Gregg Toland) and *Ambersons* (Stanley Cortez), the overlapping conversations, the heavy contrasts of light and shadow, with faces emerging, white and isolated, from a chiaroscuro of darkness – these are the devices any film-maker can borrow, and any number have. But no one but Welles can make a Welles film, even if (as in the opening sequence of *Lolita*) imitation of the style can take on a style of its own.

From the authority of a William Randolph Hearst to that of a small-town police chief, Welles has been fascinated by the power that corrupts, the shadow landscape across which move men like his own Harry Lime. He films up to his own size, which is considerable; he needs more to make a film *with* than his nervous backers, at most stages in his career, have been prepared to give him. So, across the years, stretches the trail of films announced but never begun, or begun but never completed, the tantalizing possibilities far outweighing in number the actual films that exist on the screen, while Welles the director has remained inactive and Welles the actor has been lending his own arrogant authority to any part, from Clarence Darrow to Benjamin Franklin to Cesare Borgia. It would be too simple, though, to see Welles as the victim of an implacable industrial system. *Kane* and *The Magnificent Ambersons* are there; and the Hollywood of twenty years ago stood by and allowed Welles to pack more of himself into these two films than most men would into twenty. Now Hollywood is an industry which hardly knows where its next blockbuster is coming from, and the innovations are being made in Europe. But Welles, like his films, is still there; the man on the cinema's conscience, but also the man who would fit into any production system like a rogue elephant into a circus procession.

12. Looking for an Audience

Orson Welles has praised *Marienbad* in a television interview, although it is a film which he does not personally like, because of the doors it opens: the fact that a film like this can be made, and can find its international public, is a sign of the improving times for the film-maker. Meanwhile John Houseman, one of the most experienced and intelligent of Hollywood producers, admits that

The real problem with American films today is who you are making them for. . . . Most of us face this harassing dilemma that we are working in a mass medium that has lost its mass audience and won't admit it.

Two statements, coming from different areas of film-making, complement rather than contradict each other; and between them they indicate something of the change which has overtaken the cinema within the last few years.

It is almost impossible, in this medium, to draw clear distinctions between an economic problem and an artistic one: the two things are inextricably linked together, and in general terms one could say that a minority cinema has been a luxury only a healthy majority cinema could afford. Set aside the moments of high national tension and urgency, which stimulate film-making such as you got in Russia during the twenties or in Italy just after the war, and it is apparent that the commercially buoyant cinema, working for a large and automatic audience, is also the one that can afford to take chances. As in publishing, the best-sellers help to finance the rest. This, at least, made sense until a few years ago. Now we have a rather different situation: an economic crisis which the art-house film, that frail and delicate creature, is surviving not too badly, on its own terms, while the average entertainment movies have run into trouble. Admittedly, the scale of the two operations is not comparable: a film made by Truffaut or Bergman or Antonioni does not even have to approach the earnings of one made by Minnelli or Cukor or Hitchcock. A specialized distributor, acquiring the rights of a film for the British market, thinks in terms of a guarantee of only a few thousand pounds. But this audience is an international one, steadily on the increase, and well worth the commercial trouble of European if not Hollywood film-makers. So far, so good; but no one with any concern for the cinema would happily see it go too far. An art-house cinema is a fine thing: an all art-house cinema would be a catastrophe. The cinema is not just Welles and Buñuel and Bresson, but whatever people are prepared to queue up for on a wet Saturday night. It is in the Odeons that the myths are made, the popular history of the cinema written; and it is in the Odeons that the future of the mass medium, the closest that the twentieth century has come to a popular art of its own haphazard and improvident making, must be decided.

Who now goes to the cinema in Britain? The figures are all too clearly charted. From an exceptional 1,635 million admissions in 1946, to 1,396 million in 1950, to 515 million in 1960, to 415 million in 1962, the line goes steadily down. Just as in America the battle with television was intensified about 1951 when TV for the first time linked the entire United States, so in

Britain the real slide in attendance figures dates from the mid fifties, when television sets were being bought at top speed by the working classes and also (coincidentally or not) when commercial television came into being.

At present, the weekly cinema audience is slightly under 8 million, averaged out over the year, although in the bleak month of December 1962 the figure dropped to a melancholy 5.9 million. By most reasonable standards, this still seems enough of a mass audience, until one glances across at television to see what the real mass public looks like, and remembers some of the more ironic statistics. The B.B.C. counts on an audience of about three million for its 'Cinema Today' programmes, dealing with a fairly esoteric and specialized range of subjects; an estimated five million watched the TV screening of Eisenstein's *Ivan the Terrible*, a fine figure to set against the few hundred thousand, at the most, who can have seen the film in the cinemas. If some of the audience which watches movies so indiscriminately at home went to the cinema instead, then the problems of the industry would be solved. Failing that, producers are prepared to pursue them into their homes by way of Pay Television.

Pay Television divides the film industry: producers are inclined to support it (how else, said Sir Michael Balcon in a letter to *The Times*, can they rediscover their adult audience, now assumed to be at home in front of their television sets?); exhibitors on the whole oppose it, for reasons sufficiently obvious. Given a large enough Pay TV network, a film-maker might reckon to get back a good part of his total costs in a few evenings, at the same time bypassing all the very sizeable expenditure of mass distribution through cinemas. Clearly it is a dream, of a kind; but the whole case for Pay TV still, at the time of writing, remains to be fought out, and on much wider grounds than these. No one can expect really to know the answers until the system has been tested in practice, not as a novel and isolated experiment but as a genuine alternative to existing fashions in entertainment. Undeniably, a film made for the cinema does not look half as good on a 21-inch screen, and the idea of the cinema as a sort of sub-section of television, kept going by courtesy of the small screen, encouraged perhaps to scamp on technical niceties because on television these are less likely to show, might turn out to be going after an audience the hard way. Mr John Spraos, economist and author of a book with the bleak if incontrovertible title *The Decline of the Cinema*, has forecast one possible outcome of a licensed system of Pay TV in terms that demand quotation:

With Toll-TV offering an outlet of comparable, or perhaps greater profitability, the cinemas will be up against films by the fireside which are either identical with those they are themselves exhibiting or very close substitutes. . . . In that event, perhaps no more than 100 to 200 cinemas in key population centres will survive, living on a diet of super-spectaculars. . . . Coach parties from far and wide will converge upon such cinemas, and seats might have to be booked months ahead where a film which outspectacles the common run of spectaculars is put on show. Nine out of ten films shown in these cinemas will be American, and the tenth almost certainly not British (as distinct from expatriate American) unless the financial structure of production in this country is revolutionized to make the shooting of spectaculars possible.

These are highly controversial suggestions, by no means accepted by most sections of the film industry. Few people would probably really want a situation in which going to the cinema meant either boarding a bus to see the 1970 equivalent of *Ben-Hur* or *South Pacific* or *The Longest Day*, or dropping a coin in the TV slot. But as the audience declines (and Mr Spraos has conjectured that by 1970 there might be, conceivably, a further twenty-five-per-cent drop on the 1960 figure), so, inevitably, the cinemas shut their doors. Between 1957 and 1963 over a third of the cinemas in the United Kingdom went out of business, leav-

ing fewer than 2,500 in operation. And, as Mr Spraos empha-
sizes, this policy of shut-down, euphemistically known to the
industry as rationalization, may itself contribute to the situation
which brings it about. If the nearest surviving cinema is five
miles or more away, at the end of a poorly served bus-route, then
who will make the necessary effort to go to it? *The Decline of the
Cinema*, in fact, puts up a case for some form of aid to the exhibition side of the industry, on the grounds that the local cinema is
a social amenity of which people ought not in fairness to be
deprived. The 'curtailment of available facilities for cinema-
going', we are told, brings about a forced abstention, which is
not the consequence of 'some independent shift in tastes towards
alternative entertainment'.

Again, the case can be argued either way, though no one
would expect the film companies, unaided, to keep unprofitable
cinemas open as a philanthropic exercise. They have a large
enough problem of empty seats confronting them without that.
The pulling down of two big London cinemas, the Empire and
the Gaumont, and the reconstruction of smaller theatres within
buildings used for other purposes, clearly points one way forward. But while the major circuits controlled by Rank and
Associated British can regroup and reorganize, sell some cinemas, convert others, and close down in cases where one cinema
has been undercutting the trade of another, the small independent exhibitor has no choice but to go out of business, to sell up
the backstreet cinema with its atmosphere of draughts and
disinfectant, layers of old posters superimposed one on top of
another, and twice-weekly changes of extraordinary double-
feature programmes. There, at last, goes part of the long childhood of the cinema.

It goes with its audience, which never cared too much what
was on the screen, sat through the films so worn by constant projection that the action offered an involuntary jump cut on every
reel change, and asked of the cinema little more than that it

remember to change its programmes twice a week. Now this audience is watching 'Coronation Street' and 'Compact', and amiably giving its attention, on television, to anything from Rogers and Astaire, to the Warner Brothers post-war thrillers, to the cinema-weary second features long ago put safely out to grass and now haphazardly rescued from retirement. When the B.B.C. puts on a Saturday-night film – any film, it appears – it can safely count on an audience a great deal larger than that attracted by all the new films showing in all the cinemas in the country during the entire week.

If the cinema has lost its habit audience, whom has it kept? The most reliable statistical breakdown is probably that provided by the Screen Advertisers Association, which analyses audience figures (1961 is the most recent year available) in terms of district, class, and age for the benefit of advertisers. The proportion of cinemagoers in the total adult population, they find, varies from fifty-two per cent in London to thirty-two per cent in the Anglia TV region; the average number of cinema visits a year from twenty-seven in Scotland (the London figure is only twenty-one) to twenty in the Midlands. If you go to the cinema at all, in other words, you probably go roughly once a fortnight. Of the total audience over sixteen years of age, sixty per cent comes within the sixteen to twenty-four age-group, with the rate of attendance falling away all the time as the age-graph rises. Finally, there is the income background, in terms of the advertisers' customary breakdown: AB (upper and upper middle class); C1 (lower middle class); C2 (skilled working class); DE (working class and people on the lowest subsistence level). By this reckoning, we find that 168·6 million cinema admissions in 1961 came from the DE class; 121·5 million from C2, 80·5 million from C1, and only 28 million from AB. Or, to put it rather more manageably, we have an adult cinema-going public of which not much less than three-quarters is working class. Statistics provide the background to the problems of the industry. It knows the audience it has; it tries, in devious and obvious ways, to keep them; and it knows the audience it has not got, the people who go to the cinema not at all, or so infrequently that their presence cannot be reckoned on the graphs; the people who turn out to make a *West Side Story* or a *Lawrence of Arabia* or a *Longest Day* one kind of success and a *Dolce Vita* another; the people every film producer is out to catch (indeed, *must* catch) when he invests a great deal of money in a movie.

In default of this audience, the cinema has turned, hopefully or desperately, to its teenagers. During the war, the film public could be taken to include pretty well everybody, which gave it a natural bias towards middle-age. It was not the teenagers who made Betty Grable the forces' pin-up, or suffered with a Joan Crawford compelled to do the washing-up or a Bette Davis released by psychiatry from cardigans and cotton stockings. The popular musicals (American) worked through the careers of the song-writers of the twenties and thirties, assuming a ready nostalgia in their audience; the popular musicals (English) sent Anna Neagle tripping through Mayfair. If this cinema had any image of its audience in mind, it must have been of a woman with a shopping basket, out for a rejuvenating afternoon with the stars.

But, as the age-level of the audience has fallen, so the films have gone out to meet it. We have had the rock films and the twist films and the hey-day of Elvis Presley; Hollywood has offered us *Hot Rod Girl, Dragstrip Girl, Reform School Girl, High School Confidential, School for Violence, Monster on the Campus*, and that ultimate fantasy *I Was a Teenage Werewolf*; the misunderstood adolescence theme is always with us, from Culver City to Tokyo. Efforts to cultivate the teenage audience have sent middle-aged film-makers out on forlorn expeditions into the hot-rod and Espresso territory; or have encouraged them to flirt naïvely with the censor, to put on displays of self-conscious daring intended to suggest that their really rather respectable wares are a sort of cinematic equivalent to reefer cigarettes.

The shoddiness of a lot of entertainment film-making can be explained in these terms: there are plenty of people around trying to gauge what teenagers want, and making some strident or pitiful or plainly silly bids for their attention. From another angle, though, it is the young audience which put the *nouvelle vague* commercially on its feet in France, which shows itself no less receptive to *Saturday Night and Sunday Morning* than to *It's Trad, Dad*, which helps the cinema to junk some of its wearier conventions. The pursuit of the teenager has not been a dead loss; and, in any case, it engages the full-time attention of only a few. To be really successful, a film has still to cut across all the barriers of age and class and nationality, whether it fills the world's specialized cinemas (like a *Jules et Jim* or a *L'Avventura*), or runs for four years in a single cinema (like *South Pacific*), or floods the mass market in a short, sharp exploitation campaign (like *Hercules Unchained* or *Dr No*). The fortunes of the production sector of the industry are riding with the few films that achieve this rather than the many that do not. Everyone knows that more than half the movies going into production in Hollywood or Rome, London or Paris, are likely to end up on the wrong side of the balance sheet; everyone hopes that it will not happen to his picture; and a few very shrewd men (a producer like Dino de Laurentiis, said never to have lost money on a picture, or Walt Disney) can still be pretty confident that it will not. Before the war, when audience taste could be gauged with tolerable accuracy, a few films did spectacularly well, a few did extremely badly, and most paid their way. Now, as in the theatre, the gap between failure and success widens every year, and the cinema rides a spectacular switchback, with its talents fighting to hang on around the curves.

Within the next decade, we are likely to see the business position clarified: Pay Television (probably, in some form); a number of strategically sited big cinemas, showing films in Cinerama or in one of the 70 mm. processes; and a range of small cinemas, some art houses, some not, which would not necessarily be tied to a weekly-release system which assumes that in the eyes of the box-office all films are equal. Shorn of too many over-large cinemas, the legacy of the thirties, the industry can come to grips with the realities of its audience. Even at the lowest estimate, this will remain a public worth fighting for.

But the economics of the business still hinge on the primary question of what people are going to pay to see. When a star is reported to be getting $1,000,000 for a picture, or a director $100,000, and columnists open fire with comparisons with nurses' salaries or prime ministers' salaries, does the figure represent the real value of her box-office drawing power or his professional skill? Does anyone know? One of the odd things about the cinema industry has been that it treats its products like merchandise without going in for the kind of market research which might give it a clearer lead. Admittedly, there are problems. Ask people in advance if they would choose to see a film starring X and Y, on such and such a subject and with such and such a title, and they will give you a series of amiable affirmatives. Actually make the film, to these specifications, and they will stay away. Hollywood, at various times in its history, has tried this kind of pre-testing of reactions, to remarkably little effect. The alternative is the kind of desperate chopping and changing which may go on after a sneak preview, when a bad audience response (as in the case of John Huston's *The Red Badge of Courage*) brings on an attack of nerves. But the wider and more general questions, of what audiences want from the cinema, and what they think they are getting, and how they like it, habitually find their answers in clichés. Every so often we are told that the story now counts for more than the stars, with the suggestion that this marks some kind of progress in public taste. Meanwhile, producers employ smash-and-grab tactics in their pursuit of any star whose name means anything commercially, agents force up their clients' salaries, and the stars get away with temperamental outbursts so awe-inspiring as at least to indicate their own confidence that the business could never survive without them.

Anomalies flourish in this undisciplined industry, one of them being the way distinctions seem to get drawn between commercial and non-commercial enterprises. To the uninitiated, a commercial film might seem to be one which actually makes money. In fact, a producer can survive a formidable series of flops provided it is recognized that his pictures were *intended* to make money. The producer whose pictures are regarded as uncommercial (that is to say, are patently made with financial profit as a secondary rather than a primary motive) is, paradoxically, the one who has to keep his head financially above water if he intends to stay in business.

In fact, and inevitably, all but amateur films are made with a greater or lesser degree of commercial motive. The cost of producing any kind of film whatsoever, on anything approaching a professional scale, imposes the necessity to find an audience. And although everyone agrees, in theoretical terms, that film-making has become too expensive, in an inflationary period no one has been able to do much about it. £20,000 will buy you a second feature in Britain and a first feature in some industries less highly organized; for £120,000 you can get *Saturday Night and Sunday Morning*; for £500,000 a costume spectacle (*Tom Jones*) in England or a fairly modest studio picture (*All Fall Down*) in America; for £2,000,000 you can have *The Guns of Navarone*; for £6,000,000 or £7,000,000 the blockbuster, *Mutiny on the Bounty* class, and for £12,000,000 or so *Cleopatra*. Above a certain level grandiosity sets in, and a million or more begins to seem a matter of concern mainly to the accountants. And this relates only to the bare negative cost of the film. On top come all the expenses incurred in merchandising, the advertising, the promotion, the print costs. A picture's basic budget, too, will encompass so many ancillary expenses, studio overheads, financial charges, interest payments, insurance coverage, and so forth, that within any given production system costs are automatically likely to be forced up to a certain level.

Yet the very expensive film, with rare exceptions, has managed to justify itself at the box-office; as indeed it must do. One of the laws of film-making has been that if you can afford to spend enough, you ought to be able to get it back again. If you march 10,000 men up and down a hill, with a Charlton Heston to lead them, throw in a not too disruptive orgy here and a little torture there, employ sufficiently celebrated writers to hammer out the dialogue, cart tons of scenery around the world, building roads if necessary to transport it, film the whole thing in Super Technirama 70 and throw in an extra half-million dollars for the publicity, then it would be a heartless public which failed to respond. Lower down the financial scale, where everything becomes a gamble, the cinema must still sign up the stars television cannot buy, go to the places television cannot reach, exploit its colour and the size of its screens. Film units go on safari in Africa or vanish into the Australian bush; on every view in Europe which has ever caught a tourist's fleeting attention, a movie camera will sooner or later be focused.

The economic necessity for this – or at any rate the economic justification – is plain to see; the artistic necessity is not. Too many good film-makers are engaged, too much of the time, on projects which patently leave them apathetic, disenchanted, endeavouring to whip up an excitement they cannot share for an audience about whose existence they remain uncertain. The whole popular art aspect of the cinema, the myths and the folklore, depends on a ready and creative interplay between screen and audience: myths are offered and accepted; conventions built up and recognized; a current runs between mass medium and mass public, and audiences know where they are and what they expect. An industry which is compelled to break this current, to pull the switch, will continue to supply popular entertainment, good, bad, and indifferent, but will make of it something more impersonal, something the audience finds it easier to take or leave, on its own capricious terms.

As films get bigger, so they pass out of the area of one man's creative control. In *Ben-Hur* an expert was called in to stage the chariot race; in *The Longest Day*, Darryl Zanuck commanded the work of three directors. There is no reason why this practice should not increase, why if a film takes as long to construct as a factory or a stretch of motorway, and costs not much less, it should not employ as many specialized talents under a general coordinating hand. But as films get bigger, so, by a logical and inevitable reaction, other people begin thinking in other terms. And one has the ultimate paradox: a big box-office cinema which can hardly afford to speak too personally, for fear of losing its audience, and a minority cinema which cannot afford to speak in any way but personally, for fear of losing *its* audience.

Traditionally, through its conditions of exhibition if for no other reason, this has been a medium of public statement. In so far as the artist thinks at all of the people he is addressing, it must be of a crowd sitting in the darkness, held by flickering images projected on a screen, reacting to a collective experience. Where the novelist's relationship with the reader can be private, an imposition of will, an interplay of minds, an encounter between one sensibility and another, the cinema assumes the presence of its audience – as, indeed, did the novel itself a hundred years ago, when reading aloud was still in fashion.

There are certain films, comedies most obviously, which can hardly be enjoyed without an audience. They may, indeed, be made with its presence very specifically in mind, cut to allow pauses between the gags, time for a large audience to laugh, collect itself, settle down to prepare for the next joke. In the old days of Hollywood's precision film-making, if ninety laughs were counted at the sneak preview, then ninety laughs, appropriately spaced, were what the movie was held to offer. A thriller, equally clearly, needs an audience: the Hitchcock suspense sequence, watched on an editola, looks like a piece of machinery, a stripped-down section of an engine. See it in a cinema, and the tension flows between screen and spectators.

One takes this for granted, as one does all those familiar conventions which the cinema developed over the years to help the audience to get its bearings: that old calendar, with the torn leaves fluttering away, which used to be such a standby for the passing of time; the endless train wheels for journeys; the Eiffel Tower for Paris and Trafalgar Square for London; all the apparatus brought into play to introduce a flashback. And now increasingly, in France and Italy and to some extent America, we have the films which make hay with the conventions, the films conceived as personal statements, which we may watch with other people in a cinema or by ourselves in a viewing theatre, or on a television screen, the films which insist that *we* keep up with *them*, and which consequently are bound, by their density or their subtlety, their allusiveness or their technical unfamiliarity, to leave part of their audience behind. The gap has always been there: as wide between *Zéro de Conduite* and *It Happened One Night*, or *Les Dames du Bois de Boulogne* and *The Best Years of Our Lives*, as between *Marienbad* and *Lawrence of Arabia*. The difference is in two things: the number of people, all over the world, who now see what twenty or thirty years ago would have been thought of as defiant minority films; and the number of film-makers very consciously concerned with the language of the screen. We have a new public for something vaguely called a new cinema, spreading out from the specialized cinemas and the film societies, but also coming in from the Odeons and the Gaumonts. The movies have never found it easier to get an audience for work with genuine minority appeal or genuine mass appeal; and as long as that lasts, we may quite well be experiencing the decline of the cinema and, at the same time, the rise of the film.

13. Towards a New Cinema

New cinema, new wave, new American cinema, Italian renaissance: the phrases crop up, forming a convenient kind of critical shorthand, which like most shorthand can only be effectively read back by the writer. Of course nothing is really new, so that antecedents can always be traced, ancestors run to earth; and of course new waves all too soon begin to look like tired conventions. One thing, however, seems certain. In the doldrums of the middle fifties, it would have been difficult to write a survey of this kind without casting sneaking glances over one's shoulder towards the supposed golden ages of film-making. Neo-realism was dying with the whimper of an *Il Tetto*, British cinema somnolent, the French industry given over to a professionalism that masked an absence of original thought, Hollywood still narcissistically enchanted by the size of its own screens. Lethargy seemed to be creeping up, as though the cinema felt television closing up on it and had half-hearted ideas of conceding the race. Now, looking back, the period around 1956 seems a watershed: between the neo-realists and the *nouvelle vague*, or (and this is not simply another way of saying the same thing) between a middle-aged cinema and a young one.

It was certainly time some of the rules were broken, technically as well as aesthetically. Raoul Coutard, the brilliant French cameraman, shoots straight into the light in *Lola*; the ubiquitous hand-held camera gets close in among the crowds; *Hiroshima mon Amour* obliterates the flashback; Antonioni takes over a golf club to shoot part of *La Notte*; Woodfall rents a house for *A Taste of Honey*; everyone, everywhere, discovers the advantage of making films outside studios, so avoiding that systematization which manages to impose the same kind of technical stamp on each and every subject. What the cinema of the middle fifties needed, to shake it up, was some artists prepared to have a go, to smash up a few conventions just to see what the pieces looked like. The fact that it found them, in France, spurred on other people. Everyone wanted a *nouvelle vague*, even if the French decided, as soon as they had it, that they were not entirely sure what they had got hold of. As a result, and to an extent unthinkable only a few years ago, we are living in the age of the first film. Godard, Truffaut, Varda, Demy, Pasolini, Olmi, Patroni Griffi, Polanski, Reisz, Schlesinger, Cassavetes: none of these have had to serve an apprenticeship in B-features, to await the moment of critical recognition. Festival entries tend to be divided between the films of the cinema's great and now ageing artists (Renoir, Buñuel, Ozu), of its post-war generation (Antonioni, Wajda, Torre Nilsson, Bergman) and of its established and unestablished newcomers. Missing, on the whole, is the generation from the first decade of sound.

As always, the reaction is against the recent past. But although there is something just tangible enough to be called a new way of looking at the cinema, there certainly is no such thing as a collective spirit. Any generalization based on one group of films can be smartly cancelled out on the evidence of another. If there is no common ground between, say, Godard and Antonioni, there is not much more between Godard and Resnais, his fellow-countryman. But *some* movies, it can be said, are more spontaneous than they used to be, more inclined to snatch at the fleeting moment; they relish ambiguity, the kind of Pirandellian situations in which characters are always going in search of their own identities, are not even entirely sure where life ends and film begins; they are based on a knowledge of the cinema's past which enables them to use quotation and allusion, to work within a frame of reference necessary to the creators if sometimes perplexing to the audience; they look as though the people making them enjoyed what they were doing; and they admit their own imperfections.

Should one [to quote Truffaut] continue to pretend to be telling a story which is controlled and authoritative, weighted with the same meaning and interest for the film-maker and for the spectator? Or ought one rather to admit that one is throwing on the market a kind of rough draft of one's ideal film, hoping that it will help one advance in the practice of this terribly difficult art?

Any number of young artists are engaged in this exploration; and are assuming, as directors have not been able to do on this scale since the twenties, that they have a right of discovery, that the whole industrial framework of studios and big companies ought not to stand in their way. In America, inevitably, the problem comes most clearly into focus. From a round-table discussion published in the Californian magazine *Film Quarterly*, one extracts two quotations. According to the producer John Houseman:

Think how very few American films, even among the good ones, have a signature. This has something to do with the organization of the studios and the releasing companies, but it also has a lot to do with the audience. There is a very strong resistance to individual statements in American pictures, while among the worst European film-makers there is nearly always some kind of personal statement.

From Irvin Kershner, one of the younger American directors:

How do you make a film which is entertaining, which has ideas, which is let's say adult, which doesn't depend on violence for its shock, doesn't depend on sex for its excitement – how do you create this kind of drama for $200,000 when there's no time to play, to waste, to take a chance, to do all the things that an artist has to do to make a film?

The director is talking practically, in terms of the low-budget film made within the industrial system, and the producer theoretically. But both are preoccupied with this question of a 'signature', of the stamp of personality as something which ought to be burnt into a film. A few years ago, in a Hollywood more easily confident of its own considerable assets, the distinction between one kind of movie and another might have been taken for granted, or at least accepted as a fact of cinema life. Now it has to be argued out, with the implication, which by no means all Europeans would subscribe to, that Europe has got the upper hand.

An answer, of a sort, is to work outside the studios; and within the last few years there has been a good deal of talk about a new American cinema, New York based, independent, radically minded. Some critics have resolutely battled to extract evidence of a 'movement' from films made in half a dozen styles: from Lionel Rogosin's dramatized documentary of Skid Row, *On the Bowery*, to John Cassavetes's improvised actors' exercise, *Shadows*; from Shirley Clarke's *The Connection*, which wraps its study of junkies waiting for a fix within the elaborate protective cocoon of a film within a film, to Richard Leacock's television documentaries, where a remorseless camera moves close in on a football match or an election meeting; from the short-film work of numerous *avant-garde* experimentalists to the low-budget features with a toe-hold in the commercial market.

Jonas Mekas, a New York critic and one of the most energetic propagandists for this whole elusive idea of a new American cinema, sees it as:

an ethical movement, a human act. . . . It was in his quest for inner freedom that the new artist came to improvisation. The young American film-maker, like the young painter, musician, actor, resists his society. . . . He cannot arrive at any true creation by reworking and rehashing ideas, images and feelings that are dead and inflated – he has to descend much deeper, below all that clutter. His spontaneity, his anarchy, even his passivity, are his acts of freedom. [Further, argues Mekas] . . . If we study the modern film poetry, we find that even the mistakes, the out-of-focus shots, the shaky shots, the unsure steps, the hesitant movements, the over-exposed, the under-exposed bits, have become part of the new cinema vocabulary, *being part of the psychological and visual reality of modern man* [my italics].

Part of the vocabulary these things certainly are, though in employing resounding theory in defence of practical inadequacy, Jonas Mekas hardly makes the out-of-focus shots seem any less blurred. A shaky camera is much more likely to be evidence of financial stringency or practical inexperience than of sincerity. But it becomes very easy to get into a state of mind in which roughness is equated with honesty, in which the more raw and unfinished and obviously unprofessional a film looks, the more fervently it will be held to be asserting its independence. (Then, unfairly, Hollywood strikes back by trying to give some of its movies the fashionable grainy look of hard actuality.)

Resistance to Hollywood's pluperfect technique, precisely because it is Hollywood, and professional, and expensive, goes with the kind of unfocused protest against society and its works which turns a film such as Mekas's own *Guns of the Trees* into a tirade of outrage. Here the Americans part company with the markedly unpolitical French. But they come together again in their feelings about improvisation, the value of the film which evolves its own sense of direction as it goes along. In itself, improvisation can hold a different meaning for almost any film-maker who experiments with it. Jean Rouch, in a film such as

Chronique d'un Été, uses the camera as a kind of psychiatric tool, allowing it to form a third in conversations in the belief that in its admonitory presence people are closer to revealing the truth about themselves. But he also shoots hours of footage, and it is in the editing of this that the film emerges. Truffaut and Godard improvise when it suits them. John Cassavetes, in *Shadows*, made a film which announced itself proudly as a work of total improvisation, in which the validity of any given moment depended on the degree of response the actor managed to bring to it. Improvisation may achieve that spontaneity many film-makers long for. But few directors, after all, arrive at their results through a single take, and what was spontaneous at the beginning of the day's shooting may by the end of it have become something quite different.

Advocates of improvisation, though, are much more concerned with the idea of release: the freeing of the actor to make contributions going beyond the range of his part, as the script records it, the freeing of the camera from any rigidly preconceived plan: the freedom, in fact, to invent at the moment of shooting, to send the film off at a tangent if it seems a good idea. Many of these semi-improvised films inevitably look embarrassingly naïve: a bad actor speaking good lines is probably a happier sight than a bad actor struggling to communicate some ill-defined, ineffable inner something or other. Even when the improvised film works, as *Shadows* mostly did, it seems to do so as a once-for-all experiment, a stage in a director's career which he could not revisit if he tried, and where others follow him at their own risk. The film-maker probably has to go through technique to emerge safely on the other side, needs to know exactly what effect he's after before he sets other people loose to achieve it for him. Directors of greater *naïveté* are liable to waste as much footage on pursuing their players aimlessly around, waiting for the elusive and significant truth to hit them like a thunderbolt, as Hollywood does on tracking its stars through romantic locations. And, of course, the conventions pile up: the dead-into-camera monologues, the shots of rubbish heaps, stretches of wasteland, all the well-worn symbols of city squalor which creep like so much ivy over experimental films.

Essentially, these improvised and semi-improvised works see their function not as a controlling and shaping of experience, the discovery of a pattern or logic in a series of events, but as a baring of immediate emotion, and the shattering of expected patterns through the intervention of the haphazard and the unplanned. Art itself is a word such film-makers might not care to accept too readily, because of its connotations of tradition and discipline. A moment of direct emotional truth can bite deep beneath the surface. *Shadows* pulls off such a moment, for instance, in the needling dialogue between the white boy who has come to take the coloured girl out for the evening, the girl resentful of his colour and her own, and her two brothers. And although such piercing insights may be few and far between, and the film-maker may not always be able to regulate their coming, or to sort out the absolutely genuine from the just-off-the-mark, they are the justification of his method. Film-making, like bird-watching, creeps up on the truth.

Improvisation is a technique and a tool, and one which many contemporary film-makers reject. It is an interesting exercise to compare the published texts of such films as *L'Année dernière à Marienbad* or *L'Avventura* with the pictures themselves, to see the extent to which two films very precise in their structure had a prior existence on paper, and also to note the points at which the director has moved away from the original text. Film-making is not an exact science: areas for improvisation always remain open. The creative process is continuous, from the thinking that goes on before the film actually goes into production, to the changes in the original conception effected at the shooting stage, to the final shaping of the picture during the editing.

'I go away by myself for half an hour or so before we begin

shooting', says Antonioni, and 'you might say I was inventing a little bit of film.'

'I arrive in the morning knowing what I intend to do during the day, but not how I intend to do it,' says Bresson.

'I have an idea at the back of my mind, and I develop it with my actors; although we work from a written text, the dialogue may only be put down on paper a few minutes before we start filming,' says Godard.

Use of actual locations, for interior as well as exterior scenes, has also cut down on some of the elaborate pre-planning customary where sets have to be constructed to order in the studio.

Another pointer for the new cinema, and one which links directors who otherwise have little in common, is the kind of relationship the film-maker assumes with his audience. Increasingly, he tells them as much as he cares to, and they take it from there. When one talks of the film as moving closer to the novel, this is to some extent what one means: that it addresses itself to each of us as an individual, that it deals in ambiguities of motivation and relationship which it is for us to elucidate, that it assumes our familiarity with the grammar of the screen. What does it mean? It means what you think it means. 'Am I to sympathize with this character or not?' – 'I've shown him to you as I see him, now it's for you to make up your mind.' This is the sort of dialogue set up between spectator and director. Why does Anna disappear in *L'Avventura*, and what has happened to her? Have the man and the woman in *L'Année dernière* met last year, or this year, or never? Why does Patricia betray Michel in *À Bout de Souffle*, and what are we to make of her last enigmatic close-up? Why does Jeanne Moreau drive her car off the broken bridge in *Jules et Jim*? Are the various women we encounter in *Lola* meant to express aspects of Lola herself – Lola as she was, as she will be, as she might have been? Audiences may ask the questions, and critics speculate, at enormous length, about the answers. The directors concerned know that they have made the questions irrelevant, or have answered them to their own satisfaction.

It would not do to make too much of this: the cinema is in no danger of becoming as esoteric as all that. But it is, on a previously unprecedented scale, testing out some of its own powers, its ability to move freely in time as well as space, its ability to withhold as well as to deliver information, to surprise, and confuse. In Roger Leenhardt's *Rendezvous de Minuit* there is a café episode in which the conversation turns on the possibility that one of the new film-makers, from the shelter of a newspaper kiosk, is at that moment turning a hidden camera on the scene. A joke; a critic's conceit (Leenhardt is critic as well as film-maker); an affectation; and also a comment by the cinema on the cinema, on its determination that we should take it on its own terms, remember that we are sitting in a theatre watching a film, and adjust our conception of reality to admit that in the present-tense grammar of the movies there is only the reality of what is *now* on the screen.

Whether all this should be regarded as merely fashionable, or as symptomatic of the way art reacts to a disordered and confused society, a world in which areas of certainty contract and judgements become relative, it certainly relates to another trend in contemporary film-making. A reaction has set in against the cinema of straightforward social purpose, and a *Grapes of Wrath* or a *Bicycle Thieves*, a *Stars Look Down* or a *Terra Trema*, is not very likely to be made today by any of the major film-makers in the West. Underlying many of the really significant films of the last few years is an unspoken sense that the public context, the social scene in all its complexity, is something too big to grasp and too unwieldy to be susceptible to change. We have a cinema of personal relationships, private worlds, and anti-heroes engaged in splicing together the broken and rough ends of personality, or in pursuing illusions half-recognized as such; an amoral cinema, or one endeavouring to construct its morality through a series of *ad hoc* judgements. *Hiroshima mon Amour* is not about peace or the Bomb, as much as it is about a woman trying to live with her past; *Shadows* is not about the colour question, as much as it is about a coloured family whose attitudes to each other are at least as relevant as their feelings about the way the world treats them; *À Bout de Souffle* is not about crime, but about Jean-Paul Belmondo and Jean Seberg; *La Notte* is not a tract on modern marriage. Within their context, these films are not uncommitted or disengaged works, but their commitments remain essentially to individuals. Any generalizations we care to make really become our own affair; and the films accept no responsibility (as did *The Grapes of Wrath* or *Bicycle Thieves*) to offer them on our behalf.

In an essay on the novel, Mary McCarthy has complained that what modern fiction lacks is the factual context: the calm, detailed, *interested* description of how factories are run, how a town is put together as a social organism, the accumulation of facts about freemasonry or whaling or the Chancery Courts, which characterized the nineteenth-century novel. Elsewhere she has written:

The writer must be first of all a listener and observer, who can pay attention to reality, like an obedient pupil, and who is willing, always, to be surprised by the messages reality is sending through to him. And if he gets the messages correctly he will not have to go back and put in the symbols; he will find that the symbols are there, staring at him significantly from the commonplace.

Such comments could be applied with almost equal relevance (which is hardly surprising) to the contemporary cinema. The artist's passion for putting in the symbols, like so many currants in a cake, and the critic's for pulling them out again, rapidly enough become a bore. And the film, as well as the novel, seems to be moving away from the period when information, the assembly of facts, engaged its major artists. If the cinema robbed the novel of much of its journalism and factual reporting, television has done the same thing to the cinema.

A cinema preoccupied with personal relationships and subjective landscapes may find itself losing contact with this hard, limiting, disciplinary, and necessary world of fact. But the cinema is also a more objective medium than the novel, in the most simple sense of the novelist being able to move so exclusively into areas of subjectivity that he no longer feels any need to tell us what his people and places look like, while the film must always, and by its nature, surround its characters with the clutter of their material existence. Even if we see events through the eyes of a central character, we also remain outside him, evaluating his actions as we watch them on the screen. Even a *L'Année dernière*, with its open invitation to a subjective response, is filmed objectively. The novelist may describe a scene, and forget it: the movie can hardly get away from its own scenery.

In so much as there is a new cinema worth talking about, it is because a number of directors are very consciously thinking in terms of how screen language can be made to work for them. They are more interested in the way things look and feel and sound than in what they signify in general terms; more interested in mood than in narrative; more concerned with how people behave and give themselves away in action than with how they might choose to see themselves. They are asking from their actors not the great neon-blazing star turns but performances which break through the hard professional surface: at the worst, an emotional strip-tease; at the best, a revelation. In players such as Jeanne Moreau and Monica Vitti, Jean-Paul Belmondo and Marcello Mastroianni, they have acquired willing accomplices. Above all, they give us the sense of the film itself as a risky and unique creative adventure.

Any amount of nonsense has been produced during the last few years by directors whose main creative activity consists in taking over other people's mannerisms. Entertainment-film clichés may afford restful and tranquillizing evidence that the conventions are still in working order. New-wave clichés are deadly because they come from directors trying to pass them off as new currency. But all this was to be expected. The cinema moves a few steps closer to the minority arts: its passion for allusion and quotation, for instance, is not really very far distant from the point reached by poetry almost forty years ago; and its emphasis on the immediate can not too implausibly be related to action painting. And as it moves, so it acquires the affectations along with the advantages. Antonioni occupies the painter's traditional position: far enough back from his subject to give us our sense of dramatic distance. Some of the young French directors keep our noses pressed up against it: we can distinguish a brilliant blob of colour here, some dashing brushwork there, but if we stand a few yards back all we can see is a blurred image, with a signature scrawled boldly across the corner.

Yet the exhibitionism and self-display and dandyish conceits have been symptoms of a necessary bravado. Whatever comes out of all this restless activity of the late fifties and early sixties, in the way of durable reputations and positive advances, we are still in the middle of a whole series of uncommonly difficult transitions, as the minority film-makers move in to fill part of the gap left by the decline of the big production empires. If iconoclasm and a certain optimistic anarchy were necessary three or four years ago, a period of consolidation and sorting out now looks equally important. Can the new film-makers take enough of the audience with them? Are we likely to have, by 1970 or so, a cinema split between the mass-entertainment movies, made at huge cost for huge audiences, and the small-scale films which have left the majority audience lagging behind? It has happened in the novel, in painting, in music, and it is not inconceivable that it could happen in the cinema. Certainly one could no more expect a mass public to go every step of the way with Antonioni or Resnais or Godard, or even Truffaut despite his sensitivity to audience response, than one could have asked them to go along with Proust or Henry James or Virginia Woolf.

If the cinema had held itself down, at any given moment, to the kind of subtleties and complexities it assumed people would be able unquestioningly to follow, we would still be back with *The Great Train Robbery* and *Rescued by Rover*. But a creative cinema which leaves too much of its audience too far behind would be running a clear risk of widening the gap, already quite wide enough, between one kind of audience and another. A snobbery of the specialized cinemas can be much more debilitating and depressing than the free-for-all in which each film takes its chance with the rest. The artist who wants to put his own vision into his work is never likely to find the going entirely smooth: imagine even a Picasso who had to beg £100,000 or so before he could put paint to canvas. And the cinema enthusiasts will always be on the side of such an artist: they will look also to the takers of chances who help to keep this immensely difficult medium alive. But the showmen who found the sun shining in Los Angeles and settled down there half a century ago to make the movies were not thinking like this. They wanted the biggest audience in the world, and they got it; and along with the audience they built an art form not quite like any other.

The impulse which leads me to a Humphrey Bogart movie has little in common with the impulse which leads me to the novels of Henry James or the poetry of T. S. Eliot [wrote the American critic Robert Warshow]. That there is a connexion between the two impulses I do not doubt, but the connexion is not adequately summed up in the statement that the Bogart movie and the Eliot poem are both forms of art.

The new film-makers may be taking us that much closer to the James novel or the Eliot poem; but no one concerned about the future of the cinema, much less its past, would jettison the Bogart movie in the process. If the cinema ever goes out of business as a mass entertainment, then the fact that certain areas of experiment still remain open would be small consolation for anyone. We need the lot: films and movies, James and Bogart, minority art and mass medium. In spite of all the hazards of the last decade, which have produced so many dismal forecasts, so many pronouncements of commercial decline, it seems tolerably certain that the cinema will continue to give them to us. During the worst of its troubles, Hollywood adopted the defiant and appealing slogan 'movies are better than ever'. Oddly enough, in the long run and on a world view, the publicists may have got it about right.

Check-List of Films
and Directors

This selection of films made since the war by more than a hundred directors has been compiled by John Gillett, of the British Film Institute's Information Department, in collaboration with Penelope Houston. Without attempting to be comprehensive, it tries to cover as wide a range of feature film-making as possible, with special reference to the work of younger film-makers. Any injustices to directors of an older generation can be rectified by reference to the check-list in Roger Manvell's Pelican *The Film and the Public* (1955). We are grateful to Dr Manvell for his permission to use this as the starting-point in compiling the present list.

ALDRICH, ROBERT: *Vera Cruz*, 1954. *Kiss Me Deadly*, 1955. *The Big Knife*, 1955. *What Ever Happened to Baby Jane?*, 1962.

ANDERSON, LINDSAY: *O Dreamland*, 1954. *Thursday's Children* (with Guy Brenton), 1954. *Every Day Except Christmas*, 1957. *This Sporting Life*, 1962.

ANTONIONI, MICHELANGELO: *Cronaca di un Amore*, 1950. *La Signora senza Camelie*, 1953. *Le Amiche*, 1955. *Il Grido*, 1957. *L'Avventura*, 1960. *La Notte*, 1961. *L'Eclisse*, 1962. *Il Deserto Rosso*, 1964.

ASQUITH, ANTHONY: *The Winslow Boy*, 1949. *The Browning Version*, 1951. *The Importance of Being Earnest*, 1952. *Orders to Kill*, 1958. *The VIPs*, 1963.

ASTRUC, ALEXANDRE: *Le Rideau cramoisi*, 1953. *Les Mauvaises Rencontres*, 1955. *Une Vie*, 1958. *La Proie pour l'Ombre*, 1960. *The Pit and the Pendulum*, 1963.

AUTANT-LARA, CLAUDE: *Le Diable au Corps*, 1947. *Occupe-toi d'Amélie*, 1949. *L'Auberge rouge*, 1951. *Le Blé en Herbe*, 1953. *En Cas de Malheur*, 1958.

BARDEM, JUAN-ANTONIO: *Comicos*, 1953. *Death of a Cyclist*, 1955. *Calle Mayor*, 1956.

BECKER, JACQUES: *Antoine et Antoinette*, 1947. *Édouard et Caroline*, 1951. *Casque d'or*, 1952. *Touchez pas au Grisbi*, 1953. *Le Trou*, 1960.

BERGMAN, INGMAR: *Thirst*, 1949. *Summer Interlude*, 1950. *Summer with Monika*, 1952. *Sawdust and Tinsel*, 1953. *Smiles of a Summer Night*, 1955. *The Seventh Seal*, 1956. *Wild Strawberries*, 1957. *The Virgin Spring*, 1959. *Through a Glass Darkly*, 1961. *Winter Light*, 1962. *The Silence*, 1963.

BERLANGA, LUIS: *Welcome, Mr Marshall*, 1952. *Novio a la Vista*, 1953. *Calabuch*, 1955. *Thursday Miracles*, 1957. *El Verdugo*, 1963.

BONDARCHUK, SERGEI: *Destiny of a Man*, 1959. *War and Peace*, 1963.

BRESSON, ROBERT: *Le Journal d'un Curé de Campagne*, 1951. *Un Condamné à mort s'est échappé*, 1956. *Pickpocket*, 1959. *Procès de Jeanne d'Arc*, 1961.

BROOK, PETER: *Moderato Cantabile*, 1960. *Lord of the Flies*, 1963.

BUÑUEL, LUIS: *Los Olvidados*, 1950. *El*, 1952. *Robinson Crusoe*, 1953. *The Criminal Life of Archibaldo de la Cruz*, 1955. *Cela s'appelle l'Aurore*, 1956. *Nazarin*, 1958. *Viridiana*, 1961. *The Exterminating Angel*, 1962. *Le Journal d'une Femme de Chambre*, 1964.

CACOYANNIS, MICHAEL: *Windfall in Athens*, 1953. *Stella*, 1954. *A Girl in Black*, 1956. *A Matter of Dignity*, 1958. *Elektra*, 1961.

CAPRA, FRANK: *It's a Wonderful Life*, 1946. *State of the Union*, 1948. *Riding High*, 1950. *A Hole in the Head*, 1959.

CARNÉ, MARCEL: *Les Portes de la Nuit*, 1946. *La Marie du Port*, 1949. *Thérèse Raquin*, 1953. *Les Tricheurs*, 1958.

CASSAVETES, JOHN: *Shadows*, 1960. *Too Late Blues*, 1961.

CASTELLANI, RENATO: *Sotto il Sole di Roma*, 1948. *È Primavera* 1949. *Due Soldi di Speranza*, 1952. *Romeo and Juliet*, 1954. *Il Brigante*, 1961.

CAYATTE, ANDRÉ: *Justice est faite*, 1950. *Nous sommes tous des Assassins*, 1952. *Le Passage du Rhin*, 1960. *La Vie Conjugale*, 1964.

CHABROL, CLAUDE: *Le Beau Serge*, 1958. *Les Cousins*, 1958. *Les Bonnes Femmes*, 1960. *Landru*, 1963.

CHAPLIN, CHARLES: *Monsieur Verdoux*, 1947. *Limelight*, 1952. *A King in New York*, 1957.

CHUKRAI, GRIGORI: *The Forty-First*, 1956. *Ballad of a Soldier*, 1959. *Clear Sky*, 1961.

CLAIR RENÉ: *Le Silence est d'or*, 1947. *La Beauté du Diable*, 1950. *Les Belles de Nuit*, 1952. *Les Grandes Manœuvres*, 1955. *Porte des Lilas*, 1957. *Tout l'Or du Monde*, 1961.

CLAYTON, JACK: *Room at the Top*, 1958. *The Innocents*, 1961. *The Pumpkin Eater*, 1964.

CLÉMENT, RENÉ: *Les Maudits*, 1947. *Jeux Interdits*, 1952. *Knave of Hearts*, 1954. *Gervaise*, 1956. *Plein Soleil*, 1960. *Che Gioia Vivere*, 1961. *Le Jour et l'Heure*, 1963.

CLOUZOT, HENRI-GEORGES: *Quai des Orfèvres*, 1947. *Le Salaire de la Peur*, 1952. *Les Diaboliques*, 1954. *Le Mystère Picasso*, 1955. *La Vérité*, 1960. *Du Fond de la Nuit*, 1964.

COCTEAU, JEAN: *La Belle et la Bête* (with René Clément), 1946. *Les Parents terribles*, 1948. *Orphée*, 1950. *Le Testament d'Orphée*, 1959.

CORMAN, ROGER: *The Fall of the House of Usher*, 1960. *The Stranger*, 1961. *Tales of Terror*, 1962. *The Raven*, 1962. *The Haunted Palace*, 1963.

COTTAFAVI, VITTORIO: *Messalina*, 1960. *Hercules Conquers Atlantis*, 1961.

CUKOR, GEORGE: *Born Yesterday*, 1950. *Pat and Mike*, 1952.

The Marrying Kind, 1952. *The Actress*, 1953. *A Star is Born*, 1954. *Heller in Pink Tights*, 1959. *Let's Make Love*, 1960. *My Fair Lady*, 1964.

DASSIN, JULES: *Brute Force*, 1947. *The Naked City*, 1948. *Du Rififi chez les Hommes*, 1955. *Celui qui doit mourir*, 1957. *Never on Sunday*, 1961. *Phaedra*, 1962.

DEMY, JACQUES: *Lola*, 1960. *La Baie des Anges*, 1963. *Les Parapluies de Cherbourg*, 1964.

DONEN, STANLEY: *On the Town*, 1950, and *Singin' in the Rain*, 1952 (both with Gene Kelly). *Seven Brides for Seven Brothers*, 1954. *Funny Face*, 1956. *The Pajama Game*, 1957. *What Lola Wants*, 1958. *Charade*, 1963.

DONSKOI, MARK: *The Village Teacher*, 1947. *Mother*, 1955. *At a High Price*, 1957. *Foma Gordeyev*, 1959.

DOVZHENKO, ALEXANDER: *Poem of the Sea*, 1958. *Story of the Turbulent Years* (directed from Dovzhenko's scenarios by Julia Solntseva, his widow), 1960.

DREYER, CARL: *Ordet*, 1955.

EDWARDS, BLAKE: *Mister Cory*, 1956. *Breakfast at Tiffany's*, 1961. *Grip of Fear*, 1962. *Days of Wine and Roses*, 1962. *The Pink Panther*, 1963.

EMMER, LUCIANO: *Sunday in August*, 1950. *Leonardo da Vinci*, 1953. *Picasso*, 1954.

FABRI, ZOLTAN: *Merry-Go-Round*, 1955. *Professor Hannibal*, 1957.

FEHER, IMRE: *A Sunday Romance*, 1957.

FELLINI, FEDERICO: *Lights of Variety* (with Alberto Lattuada), 1950. *The White Sheik*, 1952. *I Vitelloni*, 1953. *La Strada*, 1954. *Notti di Cabiria*, 1957. *La Dolce Vita*, 1960. *Eight and a Half*, 1962.

FLAHERTY, ROBERT: *Louisiana Story*, 1948.

FORD, ALEKSANDER: *Five Boys From Barska Street*, 1954. *The Eighth Day of the Week*, 1958. *The Knights of the Teutonic Order*, 1960. *Cheyenne Autumn*, 1964.

FORD, JOHN: *My Darling Clementine*, 1946. *She Wore a Yellow Ribbon*, 1949. *Wagonmaster*, 1950. *The Quiet Man*, 1952. *The Sun Shines Bright*, 1953. *The Last Hurrah*, 1958. *The Horse*

Soldiers, 1959. *The Man Who Shot Liberty Valance*, 1961. *Donovan's Reef*, 1963.

FRANJU, GEORGES : *Sang des Bêtes*, 1949. *Hôtel des Invalides*, 1952. *La Tête contre les Murs*, 1958. *Les Yeux sans Visage*, 1959. *Thérèse Desqueyroux*, 1962. *Judex*, 1963.

FRANKENHEIMER, JOHN : *The Young Stranger*, 1956. *All Fall Down*, 1961. *The Manchurian Candidate*, 1962. *Seven Days in May*, 1963. *The Train*, 1964.

GODARD, JEAN-LUC : *À Bout de Souffle*, 1959. *Le Petit Soldat*, 1960. *Un Femme est une Femme*, 1961. *Vivre sa Vie*, 1962. *Les Carabiniers*, 1963. *Le Mépris*, 1963.

GOSHO, HEINOSUKE : *Four Chimneys*, 1953. *An Inn at Osaka*, 1954. *The Valley Between Life and Death*, 1954. *Growing up*, 1955.

HAMER, ROBERT : *It Always Rains on Sunday*, 1947. *Kind Hearts and Coronets*, 1949. *Father Brown*, 1954.

HAS, WOJCIECH : *Farewells*, 1958. *How to be Loved*, 1962. *Gold*, 1962.

HATHAWAY, HENRY : *The House on 92nd Street*, 1946. *Call Northside 777*, 1948. *Fourteen Hours*, 1951.

HAWKS, HOWARD : *The Big Sleep*, 1946. *Red River*, 1948. *The Big Sky*, 1952. *Monkey Business*, 1952. *Rio Bravo*, 1959. *Hatari!*, 1962. *Man's Favourite Sport*, 1963.

HEIFITZ, JOSEPH : *The Big Family*, 1954. *The Lady with the Little Dog*, 1960.

HITCHCOCK, ALFRED : *Strangers on a Train*, 1951. *Rear Window*, 1954. *The Trouble With Harry*, 1955. *The Wrong Man*, 1957. *Vertigo*, 1958. *North by Northwest*, 1959. *Psycho*, 1960. *The Birds*, 1963. *Marnie*, 1964.

HUSTON, JOHN : *The Treasure of Sierra Madre*, 1947. *We Were Strangers*, 1949. *The Asphalt Jungle*, 1950. *The Red Badge of Courage*, 1951. *The African Queen*, 1951. *Moby Dick*, 1956. *The Misfits*, 1961. *Freud*, 1962. *The List of Adrian Messenger*, 1963. *The Night of the Iguana*, 1964.

ICHIKAWA, KON : *The Burmese Harp*, 1955. *Conflagration*, 1958. *Odd Obsessions*, 1959. *Fires on the Plain*, 1959. *Bonchi*, 1960.

KALATOZOV, MIKHAIL : *The Cranes are Flying*, 1957. *The Letter That Was Not Sent*, 1959.

KÄUTNER, HELMUT : *In Jenen Tagen*, 1947. *The Last Bridge*, 1954. *The Devil's General*, 1955.

KAWALERPWICZ, JERZY : *Celluloze* (two parts), 1954. *The Shadow*, 1956. *Mother Joan of the Angels*, 1961.

KAZAN, ELIA : *Boomerang*, 1947. *Panic in the Streets*, 1950. *Viva Zapata!*, 1952. *On the Waterfront*, 1954. *Baby Doll*, 1956. *A Face in the Crowd*, 1957. *Splendour in the Grass*, 1961. *America, America*, 1963.

KELLY, GENE : *On the Town*, 1950, and *Singin' in the Rain*, 1952 (both with Stanley Donen). *Invitation to the Dance*, 1956.

KING, HENRY : *Margie*, 1946. *Twelve O'Clock High*, 1949. *The Gunfighter*, 1950. *The Bravados*, 1958.

KINOSHITA, KEISUKE : *Carmen's Pure Love*, 1952. *A Japanese Tragedy*, 1953. *The Legend of Narayama*, 1958.

KOBAYASHI, MASAKI : *The Human Condition* (trilogy), 1958 60. *Hara-Kiri*, 1962.

KOZINTSEV, GRIGORI : *Don Quixote*, 1957. *Hamlet*, 1963.

KUBRICK, STANLEY : *The Killing*, 1956. *Paths of Glory*, 1958. *Spartacus*, 1960. *Lolita*, 1962. *Dr Strangelove or: How I Learned to Stop Worrying and Love the Bomb*, 1963.

KUROSAWA, AKIRA : *Drunken Angel*, 1948. *Rashomon*, 1950. *The Idiot*, 1951. *Living*, 1952. *The Seven Samurai*, 1954. *The Lower Depths*, 1958. *Sanjuro*, 1962. *Heaven and Hell*, 1963.

LANG, FRITZ : *Clash by Night*, 1952. *The Big Heat*, 1953. *Moonfleet*, 1955. *Indian Tomb/Tiger of Eschnapur*, 1958. *The 1,000 Eyes of Dr Mabuse*, 1960.

LATTUADA, ALBERTO : *The Mill on the Po*, 1949. *Lights of Variety* (with Fellini), 1950. *Il Cappotto*, 1952. *The Unexpected*, 1961.

LEAN, DAVID : *Great Expectations*, 1946. *Oliver Twist*, 1947. *The Sound Barrier*, 1952. *Summer Madness*, 1955. *The Bridge on the River Kwai*, 1957. *Lawrence of Arabia*, 1962.

LOSEY, JOSEPH : *The Dividing Line*, 1949. *M*, 1950. *The Prowler*, 1950. *Blind Date*, 1959. *The Criminal*, 1960. *Eva*, 1962. *The Servant*, 1963.

LUMET, SIDNEY: *Twelve Angry Men*, 1957. *That Kind of Woman*, 1959. *Long Day's Journey into Night*, 1961.

MACKENDRICK, ALEXANDER: *Whisky Galore*, 1948. *The Man in the White Suit*, 1951. *Mandy*, 1952. *The Ladykillers*, 1955. *Sweet Smell of Success*, 1957. *Sammy Going South*, 1963.

MALLE, LOUIS: *L'Ascenseur pour l'Échafaud*, 1957. *Les Amants*, 1958. *Zazie dans le Métro*, 1960. *Vie privée*, 1961. *Le Feu Follet*, 1963.

MANKIEWICZ, JOSEPH: *Letter to Three Wives*, 1948. *All About Eve*, 1950. *Julius Caesar*, 1953. *Guys and Dolls*, 1955. *Suddenly Last Summer*, 1959. *Cleopatra*, 1963.

MANN, ANTHONY: *The Tall Target*, 1951. *Where the River Bends*, 1952. *Men in War*, 1957. *El Cid*, 1961. *The Fall of the Roman Empire*, 1963.

MANN, DELBERT: *Marty*, 1955. *The Bachelor Party*, 1957.

MARKER, CHRIS: *Lettre de Sibérie*, 1958. *Description d'un Combat*, 1960. *Cuba Si!*, 1961. *Le Joli Mai*, 1963. *La Jetée*, 1963.

MELVILLE, JEAN-PIERRE: *Le Silence de la Mer*, 1947. *Les Enfants terribles*, 1949. *Bob le Flambeur*, 1956. *Léon Morin, Prêtre*, 1961. *Le Doulos*, 1962. *L'Ainé des Fercheaux*, 1963.

MINNELLI, VINCENTE: *The Pirate*, 1948. *Father of the Bride*, 1950. *An American in Paris*, 1951. *The Bad and the Beautiful*, 1952. *Band Wagon*, 1953. *Lust for Life*, 1956. *Some Came Running*, 1958. *Two Weeks in Another Town*, 1962.

MIZOGUCHI, KENJI: *The Life of O-Haru*, 1952. *Ugetsu Monogatari*, 1953. *Gion Festival Music*, 1953. *Sansho Dayu*, 1954. *Chikamatsu Monogatari*, 1954. *Yokihi*, 1955. *Shin Heike Monogatari*, 1955. *Street of Shame*, 1956.

MUNK, ANDRZEJ: *Man on the Tracks*, 1956. *Eroica*, 1958. *Bad Luck*, 1960. *Passenger*, 1961.

OLIVIER, LAURENCE: *Hamlet*, 1948. *Richard III*, 1955. *The Prince and the Showgirl*, 1957.

OLMI, ERMANNO: *Time Stood Still*, 1959. *Il Posto*, 1961. *I Fidanzati*, 1963.

OPHULS, MAX: *Letter from an Unknown Woman*, 1948. *The Reckless Moment*, 1949. *La Ronde*, 1950. *Le Plaisir*, 1951. *Madame de . . .*, 1953. *Lola Montès*, 1955.

ozu, yasujiro : *The Flavour of Green Tea and Rice*, 1952. *The Tokyo Story*, 1953. *Tokyo Twilight*, 1957. *Higanbana*, 1958. *Good Morning!*, 1959. *Floating Weeds*, 1960. *Early Autumn*, 1961. *An Autumn Afternoon*, 1962.

pasolini, pierpalo : *Accattone*, 1961. *Mamma Roma*, 1962. *Rogopag* (one episode), 1963.

patroni griffi, giuseppe : *Il Mare*, 1962.

petri, elio : *L'Assassino*, 1961. *The Counted Days*, 1962.

polanski, roman : *Two Men and a Wardrobe*, 1958. *Knife in the Water*, 1962.

preminger, otto : *Daisy Kenyon*, 1947. *Bonjour Tristesse*, 1957. *Anatomy of a Murder*, 1959. *Exodus*, 1960. *Advise and Consent*, 1962. *The Cardinal*, 1963.

quine, richard : *So This is Paris*, 1954. *My Sister Eileen*, 1955. *The Solid Gold Cadillac*, 1956. *Operation Madball*, 1957. *Paris When It Sizzles*, 1963.

ray, nicholas : *They Live By Night*, 1948. *In a Lonely Place*, 1949. *The Lusty Men*, 1952. *Rebel Without a Cause*, 1955. *King of Kings*, 1961. *55 Days at Peking*, 1963.

ray, satyajit : *Pather Panchali*, 1952–5. *Aparajito*, 1957. *Jalsaghar*, 1958. *The World of Apu*, 1958. *Devi*, 1960. *Two Daughters*, 1961. *Kanchenjunga*, 1962. *Abhijan*, 1962. *Mahanagar*, 1963.

reed, carol : *Odd Man Out*, 1947. *The Fallen Idol*, 1948. *The Third Man*, 1949. *Outcast of the Islands*, 1951. *Our Man in Havana*, 1959. *The Running Man*, 1963.

reisz, karel : *We are the Lambeth Boys*, 1958. *Saturday Night and Sunday Morning*, 1960. *Night Must Fall*, 1964.

renoir, jean : *Diary of a Chambermaid*, 1946. *The River*, 1951. *The Golden Coach*, 1952. *French Can-Can*, 1955. *Le Déjeuner sur l'Herbe*, 1959. *Le Testament du Docteur Cordelier*, 1959. *Le Caporal épinglé*, 1962.

resnais, alain : *Guernica*, 1950. *Nuit et Brouillard*, 1956. *Hiroshima mon Amour*, 1959. *L'Année dernière à Marienbad*, 1961. *Muriel*, 1963.

richardson, tony : *Look Back in Anger*, 1959. *A Taste of*

Honey, 1961. *The Loneliness of the Long Distance Runner*, 1962. *Tom Jones*, 1963.

RIVETTE, JACQUES : *Paris nous appartient*, 1958–60.

ROSI, FRANCESCO : *La Sfida*, 1958. *Salvatore Giuliano*, 1961. *Le Mani sulla Città*, 1963.

ROSSELLINI, ROBERTO : *Rome, Open City*, 1945. *Paisà*, 1946. *Amore* (two parts), 1948. *Francesco, Giullare di Dio*, 1950. *Voyage in Italy*, 1954. *Il Generale della Rovere*, 1959. *Vanina Vanini*, 1961.

ROSSEN, ROBERT : *Body and Soul*, 1947. *All the King's Men*, 1949. *The Hustler*, 1961. *Lilith*, 1964.

ROSSI, FRANCO : *Friends for Life*, 1955. *Death of a Friend*, 1959.

ROUCH, JEAN : *Les Fils de l'Eau*, 1955. *Moi, un noir*, 1958. *La Pyramide humaine*, 1960. *Chronique d'un Été* (with Edgar Morin), 1961.

SAMSONOV, SERGEI : *The Grasshopper*, 1955.

SCHLESINGER, JOHN : *Terminus*, 1961. *A Kind of Loving*, 1962. *Billy Liar*, 1963.

SICA, VITTORIO DE : *Shoeshine*, 1946. *Bicycle Thieves*, 1948. *Miracle in Milan*, 1951. *Umberto D*, 1952. *L'Oro di Napoli*, 1955. *Il Tetto*, 1956. *Two Women*, 1961. *The Condemned of Altona*, 1962.

SIEGEL, DON : *Riot in Cell Block 11*, 1954. *Invasion of the Body Snatchers*, 1956. *Hell is for Heroes*, 1962.

SJÖBERG, ALF : *Miss Julie*, 1951. *Barabbas*, 1953. *Wild Birds*, 1955.

STAUDTE, WOLFGANG : *The Murderers are Amongst Us*, 1946. *Der Untertan*, 1951. *Roses for the Prosecutor*, 1959.

STEVENS, GEORGE : *A Place in the Sun*, 1951. *Shane*, 1953. *Giant*, 1956. *The Diary of Anne Frank*, 1958. *The Greatest Story Ever Told*, 1963.

STURGES, PRESTON : *Unfaithfully Yours*, 1948. *The Diary of Major Thompson*, 1955.

SUCKSDORFF, ARNE : *People in the City*, 1947. *A Divided World*, 1948. *The Great Adventure*, 1953. *A Jungle Saga*, 1958.

TASHLIN, FRANK: *Oh! For a Man*, 1957. *Cinderfella*, 1960. *Bachelor Flat*, 1961. *The Man from the Diner's Club*, 1963. *Who's Minding the Store?* 1963.

TATI, JACQUES: *Jour de Fête*, 1949. *Les Vacances de Monsieur Hulot*, 1953. *Mon Oncle*, 1958.

TORRE NILSSON, LEOPOLDO: *The House of the Angel*, 1956. *The Kidnappers*, 1958. *La Caida*, 1959. *The Hand in the Trap*, 1960. *Summer Skin*, 1961. *The Roof Garden*, 1963.

TRNKA, JIŘÍ: *The Emperor's Nightingale*, 1949. *Prince Bayaya*, 1950. *Old Czech Legends*, 1953. *A Midsummer Night's Dream*, 1959.

TRUFFAUT, FRANÇOIS: *Les Mistons*, 1957. *Les Quatre Cents Coups*, 1958. *Tirez sur le Pianiste*, 1960. *Jules et Jim*, 1961. *La Peau Douce*, 1964.

VADIM, ROGER: *Et Dieu créa la Femme*, 1956. *Sait-on jamais*, 1957. *Les Liaisons dangereuses 1960*, 1959. *Le Repos du Guerrier*, 1962. *Château en Suède*, 1963.

VARDA, AGNÈS: *La Pointe courte*, 1955. *L'Opéra mouffe*, 1958. *Du Côté de la Côte*, 1958. *Cléo de 5 à 7*, 1962.

VIDOR, KING: *Duel in the Sun*, 1947. *Beyond the Forest*, 1949. *Ruby Gentry*, 1952. *Man Without a Star*, 1955. *War and Peace* (with Mario Soldati), 1956.

VISCONTI, LUCHINO: *La Terra Trema*, 1948. *Bellissima*, 1951. *Senso*, 1954. *White Nights*, 1957. *Rocco and his Brothers*, 1960. *The Leopard*, 1963.

WAJDA, ANDRZEJ: *A Generation*, 1954. *Kanal*, 1957. *Ashes and Diamonds*, 1958. *Innocent Sorcerers*, 1960. *Samson*, 1961. *A Siberian Lady Macbeth*, 1962.

WALTERS, CHARLES: *Good News*, 1947. *Easter Parade*, 1948. *If You Feel Like Singing*, 1950. *Lili*, 1952. *The Tender Trap*, 1955. *Billy Rose's Jumbo*, 1962.

WELLES, ORSON: *Lady from Shanghai*, 1947. *Macbeth*, 1948. *Othello*, 1952. *Confidential Report*, 1955. *Touch of Evil*, 1958. *The Trial*, 1962.

WILDER, BILLY: *Sunset Boulevard*, 1950. *Ace in the Hole*, 1951. *Some Like It Hot*, 1958. *The Apartment*, 1960. *One, Two, Three*, 1961. *Irma la Douce*, 1963.

WISE, ROBERT : *The Set-Up*, 1949. *I Want to Live*, 1958. *West Side Story* (with Jerome Robbins), 1960.

WYLER, WILLIAM : *The Best Years of Our Lives*, 1946. *Carrie*, 1952. *Roman Holiday*, 1953. *The Big Country*, 1957. *Ben-Hur*, 1959. *The Loudest Whisper*, 1962.

YOUTKEVICH, SERGEI : *Othello*, 1955.

ZEMAN, KAREL : *An Invention of Destruction*, 1958. *Baron Munchausen*, 1962.

ZINNEMANN, FRED : *Act of Violence*, 1948. *The Search*, 1948. *The Men*, 1950. *Teresa*, 1951. *High Noon*, 1952. *From Here to Eternity*, 1953. *The Sundowners*, 1960. *Behold a Pale Horse*, 1964.

ZURLINI, VALERIO : *Girl with a Suitcase*, 1961. *Cronaca Familiare*, 1962.

Selected Book List

Agee, James, *Agee on Film* – vol. 1 : *Reviews and Comments*; vol. 2 : *Five Scripts*, McDowell, Obolensky, New York, 1958–60.

Alton, John, *Painting with Light*, Macmillan, New York, 1949.

Anderson, Joseph, *and* Richie, Donald, *The Japanese Film: art and industry*, Chas. E. Tuttle, Vermont, 1959.

Anderson, Lindsay, *Making a Film*, Allen and Unwin, 1952.

Aristarco, Guido, *Storia delle teoriche del film*, Einaudi, Rome, 1951.

Bazin, André, *Qu'est-ce que le cinéma?*, vols. 1–3, Éditions du Cerf, Paris, 1958, 1959, and 1961.

Béranger, Jean, *La Grande Aventure du cinéma suédois*, Le Terrain Vague, Paris, 1960.

Bergman, Ingmar, *Four Screenplays*, Secker & Warburg, 1960.

The British Film Industry, P.E.P., Report 1952 (supplement 1958).

Carrick, Edward, *Designing for Films*, Studio Press, 1949.

Clair, René, *Reflections on the Cinema*, William Kimber, 1953.

Cocteau, Jean, *Cocteau on the Film*, Dennis Dobson, 1954.

Cogley, John, *Report on Blacklisting. 1* : *The Movies*, Fund for the Republic, U.S.A., 1956.

Colpi, Henri, *Défense et illustration de la musique dans le film*, Serdoc, Lyons, 1963

Duras, Marguerite, *Hiroshima mon Amour*, Gallimard, Paris, 1961.

Eisenstein, Sergei M., *Notes of a Film Director*, Lawrence & Wishart, 1959.

Fenin, George N., *and* Everson, William K., *The Western*, Orion Press, New York, 1962.

Goodman, Ezra, *The Fifty-Year Decline and Fall of Hollywood*, Simon & Schuster, New York, 1961.

Griffith, Richard, *and* Mayer, Arthur, *The Movies*, Simon & Schuster, New York, 1957.

Halas, John, *and* Manvell, Roger, *The Technique of Film Animation*, Focal Press, 1959.

Inglis, Ruth, *Freedom of the Movies*, University of Chicago, 1947.

Jeanne, René, *and* Ford, Charles, *Cinéma d'aujourd'hui* (1945–55). *Histoire encyclopédique du cinéma*, vol. 5, S.E.D.E., Paris, 1962.

Knight, Arthur, *The Liveliest Art*, Macmillan, New York, 1957.

Kracauer, Siegfried, *Nature of Film: the Redemption of Physical Reality*, Dennis Dobson, 1961.

Kyrou, Ado, *Le Surréalisme au cinéma*, Arcannes, Paris, 1953.

Lawson, John Howard, *The Theory and Technique of Playwriting and Screenwriting*, Putnam, New York, 1949.

Leyda, Jay, *Kino*, Allen & Unwin, 1960.

Lherminier, Pierre (ed.), *L'Art du cinéma*, Seghers, Paris, 1960.

Lindgren, Ernest, *The Art of the Film*, Allen & Unwin, 1963 (revised edition).

MacCann, Richard Dyer, *Hollywood in Transition*, Houghton Mifflin, Boston, 1962.

Manvell, Roger, *Film*, Penguin Books, 1950 (revised edition). *The Film and the Public*, Penguin Books, 1955.

Manvell, Roger. *and* Huntley, John, *The Technique of Film Music*, Focal Press, 1957.

Mayer, J.P., *British Cinemas and their Audiences*, Dennis Dobson, 1948.

Morin, Edgar, *The Stars*, John Calder, 1960.

Nizhny, Vladimir, *Lessons with Eisenstein*, translated and edited by Ivor Montagu and Jay Leyda, Allen & Unwin, 1962.

Poncet, Maria Thérèse, *Dessin animé: art mondial*, Cercle du Livre, Paris, 1956.

Powdermaker, Hortense, *Hollywood – the Dream Factory*, Secker & Warburg, 1951.

Reisz, Karel, *The Technique of Film Editing*, Focal Press, 1953.

Richie, Donald, *Japanese Movies*, Japan Travel Bureau, Tokyo, 1961.

Robbe-Grillet, Alain, *Last Year at Marienbad*, John Calder, 1962.

Ross, Lillian, *Picture*, Gollancz, 1953; Penguin Books, 1963.

Ross, Lillian, *and* Ross, Helen, *The Player: a profile of an art*, Simon & Schuster, New York, 1962.

Rotha, Paul, *The Film Till Now*, Vision Press, 1960 (revised edition). *Rotha on the Film*, Faber & Faber, 1958.

Rotha, Paul, and others, *Documentary Film*, Faber & Faber, 1952 (revised edition).

Sadoul, Georges, *Histoire du cinéma*, Flammarion, Paris, 1962. *Histoire du cinéma français, 1890–1962*, Club des Éditeurs, Paris, 1962.

Seldes. Gilbert, *The Great Audience*, Viking, New York, 1950.

Seton, Marie, *Sergei M. Eisenstein: a biography*, The Bodley Head, 1952.

Siclier, Jacques, *Nouvelle Vague?*, Éditions du Cerf, Paris, 1961.

Spraos, John, *The Decline of the Cinema: an Economist's Report*, Allen & Unwin, 1962.

Talbot, Daniel (ed.), *Film: an Anthology*, Simon & Schuster, New York, 1959.

Tyler, Parker, *The Three Faces of the Film*, Thomas Yoseloff and W. H. Allen, 1960.

Warshow, Robert, *The Immediate Experience*, Doubleday, New York, 1962.

Williams, Raymond, *and* Orrom, Michael: *Preface to Film*, Film Drama, 1954.

Winnington, Richard, *Drawn and Quartered*, Saturn Press, 1948.

Wolfenstein, Martha, *and* Leites, Nathan, *Movies: a Psychological Study*, Free Press, Illinois, 1950.

Index